CW00839268

CAPOEIRA

Mestre Poncianinho
with Michelle Porter

First published in 2007 by
New Holland Publishers Ltd
London • Cape Town • Sydney • Auckland
www.newhollandpublishers.com

Garfield House
86–88 Edgware Road
London W2 2EA
United Kingdom

80 McKenzie Street
Cape Town 8001
South Africa

Unit 1, 66 Gibbes Street
Chatswood, NSW 2067
Australia

218 Lake Road
Northcote, Auckland
New Zealand

ISBN 978 1 84537 761 8

SENIOR EDITOR: Sarah Goulding
DESIGNER: Glyn Bridgewater
PHOTOGRAPHY: Mike Holdsworth
PUBLISHING MANAGER: Clare Hubbard
PUBLISHING DIRECTOR: Rosemary Wilkinson
PRODUCTION: Marion Storz

Reproduction by Pica Digital Pte Ltd, Singapore
Printed and bound in Malaysia by Times Offset (M) Sdn Bhd

2 4 6 8 10 9 7 5 3 1

DISCLAIMER

The author and publishers have made every effort to ensure that the information contained in this book was accurate at the time of going to press, and accept no responsibility for any injury or inconvenience sustained by any person using this book or following the advice provided herein.

AUTHOR'S ACKNOWLEDGEMENTS

This book would not have been possible without the help of some special people. To my students Baris Yazar, Morris Reyes, Molinha, Katie Ellwood, Isabelle Schoenholzer and Cientista — thank you for all the effort you put into your training, for the different ways you helped make this book what it is, for always being dedicated and for being my friends. Also to my best friend, Contra-Mestre Casquinha, for helping me with this book and contributing some great pictures. Thanks to my dear wife Louise Almeida who has supported and helped me in everything I do. Thanks also to Michelle Porter for her research and great writing. A big thanks to Cordão de Ouro, London, for always being with me and always supporting this beautiful and precious art of Capoeira. And the most special thanks of all to my Mestre, for teaching me the wonderful, the ever-mystifying and always revelatory art of Capoeira.

CORDAO DE OURO

CONTENTS

INTRODUCTION

I began studying Capoeira with my father in Brazil at the tender age of four, and 22 years later I am still hooked. Today Capoeira is played all over the world, and I often stop to reflect on what attracts people to this art. Since moving to London in 2000, I have taught many students from all walks of life and have travelled throughout Europe and the USA to share my passion. It is through my teaching that I have fully understood the appeal of Capoeira. People ask me why I practise it when I can never win a 'game', and I tell them that Capoeira offers much more than simply scoring points. I have seen Capoeira transform people's lives; it takes them on a journey of self development, giving them an outlet to express their individuality within the traditional framework of a martial art.

In the following pages I will outline the extraordinary history of Capoeira, from its African roots to the present day. I will also outline its development and introduce you to its most famous Mestres, Mestre Bimba and Mestre Pastinha. Music is vital within Capoeira, but confuses many who are new to the art, so I have included a section on the music and culture of Capoeira, as well as an introduction to the instruments I play. As a beginner the rules and etiquette of Capoeira may seem alien, so I have also included a section on the roda (the circle within which Capoeira is played) and the hierarchy within Capoeira. I also explain the nature of the jogo ('the game'); what it entails and how it is played. With the help of my students from the Cordão de Ouro school in London, I have broken down some of the basic moves, from the fundamental ginga, kicks, ground movements and sequences, to simple acrobatics. I have also included a brief insight into some of the more advanced moves to inspire your progress.

It would be impossible for me to cover all the possible moves within Capoeira, as these often differ from group to group. Capoeira is always growing and developing and due to the spontaneous nature of the game, new moves are developed all the time. This book is simply a guide for those wishing to explore the world of Capoeira, and I hope that it will inspire you to find a class in your area. As an instructor I can teach students the moves, the music and the tradition, but it is only by playing the game of Capoeira that you can truly express your individuality. Each Capoeirista will find their own game, and this is what makes it such a unique art. Due to the expressive nature of the art, no two schools are exactly the same, and there can sometimes be disagreements over the way things are done. I have simply shared the knowledge, experience and tradition I have been lucky enough to accumulate within Cordão de Ouro over the last 22 years. I have aimed to be true to the spirit of Capoeira, and I hope that this book inspires you. In the words of Mestre Bimba, one of the founders of modern Capoeira, 'Take what I teach you and develop it into your own reality'.

Mestre Poncianinho (Ponciano Almeida)

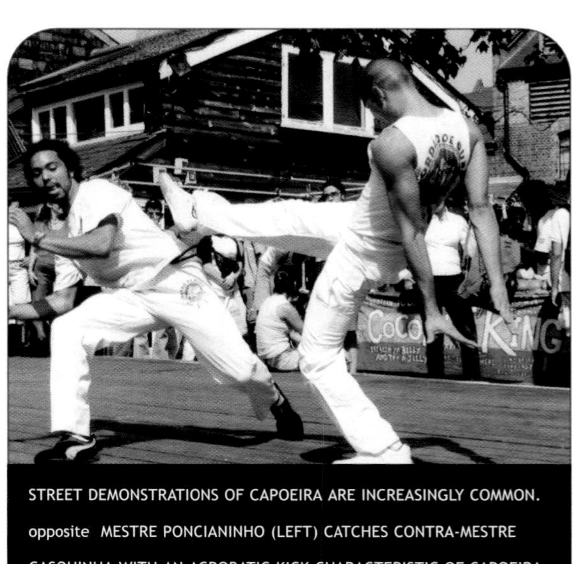

STREET DEMONSTRATIONS OF CAPOEIRA ARE INCREASINGLY COMMON.
opposite MESTRE PONCIANINHO (LEFT) CATCHES CONTRA-MESTRE CASQUINHA WITH AN ACROBATIC KICK CHARACTERISTIC OF CAPOEIRA.

What is Capoeira ?

So what is Capoeira? I am often asked to describe Capoeira, to clarify the confusion between whether or not it is a dance or a martial art. Is it a martial art for self-defence or a dance created for street performance? I will answer that it is neither, but rather a unique art that can be seen as a dance that simulates a fight, or a fight that simulates a dance. Capoeira is an expressive art and difficult to pigeonhole, as it encompasses music, fighting and fluid movements akin to a dance. A common misconception about Capoeira is that it is a non-contact sport, and some argue that it cannot therefore be a martial art. Contact does not feature heavily in Capoeira and this does indeed distinguish it from other forms of martial arts.

Each Capoeirista develops his or her own style of play, with many choosing to avoid contact altogether. A Capoeirista can choose to make contact if there is a failure in their opponent's defence, but as Capoeira does not place an emphasis on rules and point scoring, contact is not an obligatory part of the game. The way the game is played in Capoeira – the interaction between the Capoeiristas – is considered to be more important than the contact made. One does not win a game of Capoeira by making contact with the opponent, and this is what makes it unique. It should not be forgotten, however, that Capoeira was developed as a fighting art too, and can be used effectively as a form of self-defence. Some of the kicks within Capoeira can be lethal.

Why Capoeira?

The benefits of Capoeira are endless. Not only does it improve your physical strength, flexibility and reflexes, it also improves your musicality and encompasses a rich cultural and historical heritage. Many students of Capoeira learn simple Portuguese, and others take the opportunity to visit Brazil as part of their training. Capoeira is a martial art that embraces music, acrobatics, fighting, sport and philosophy. It is steeped in tradition and ritual, and works to develop the individual on both physical and mental levels.

In Capoeira one does not train alone, and the social aspect of Capoeira is one of the most appealing features of the art. Capoeira transcends all social boundaries and in Brazil, for example, you will find Capoeira academies everywhere from exclusive gyms to favelas (shanty towns). Capoeira is a democratic art, and all Capoeiristas can play together within the roda regardless of level or ability. The spirit of Capoeira can be extremely playful and does not rely on physical strength. This enables men, women and children to train and play together regardless of ability. Capoeira can accommodate both a fierce and awe-inspiring 'game' between two strong adults, or a playful exchange between father and son. Capoeira has a place for everyone who is willing to learn.

DESPITE ITS AFRICAN ROOTS, CAPOEIRA IS A BRAZILIAN MARTIAL ART.

MESTRE JOÃO PEQUENO (LEFT) AND MESTRE PAPO AMARELO, TWO WISE MASTERS OF CAPOEIRA ANGOLA ENGAGED IN A BEAUTIFUL GAME.

The history of Capoeira

Although Capoeira is a Brazilian martial art, it does not originate from the Tupi people native to Brazil, but instead has its roots firmly in African culture. There is no question as to the African roots of the art, but there is much debate as to whether or not it was imported wholesale to Brazil or developed within the senzalas (the slaves' quarters) on Brazilian soil. The argument tends to favour the theory that Capoeira was developed by African slaves within Brazil, and not brought with them as part of the cultural heritage of their homelands. This is supported by the fact that the history of Capoeira can only be linked to Brazil despite the widespread use of African slaves worldwide. The history of Capoeira, therefore, begins with the history of African slavery in Brazil.

The colonization of Brazil began in 1500 when a Portuguese fleet chanced upon her shores. The leader of the fleet, Pedro Alves Cabral, promptly declared Brazil to be the possession of the king of Portugal, and for the next three centuries she remained under Portuguese control. Brazil was colonized and exploited for economic gain, resulting in a need for an extensive labour force. Between 1540 and 1800 Brazil received in excess of two million slaves, providing labour for the coffee and sugar plantations. The first few hundred years of slavery within Brazil are poorly documented, but what is certain is that they faced cruel and intolerable treatment. What is incredible is that, in the face of such adversity and oppression, the African slaves continued to maintain a strong level of cultural identity. Even though their native songs and dances were banned by the slave owners, they still managed to keep their own traditions alive. Capoeira therefore was born under the shadow of oppression, and can be seen to represent the triumph of spirit over adversity.

The origins of the word Capoeira can also lead to much debate, and several theories exist to account for how it got its name. Many believe that the word Capoeira comes from the Tupi language and is derived from the name given to an area of jungle that has been cleared to make way for quilombos (an area of safety and hiding for fugitive slaves). The Tupi words 'caa' meaning 'down' and 'little', and 'puoera' meaning 'grass', are combined to create a word that quite literally means 'hiding in the grass'. This explanation gives credence to the underground and hidden practice of Capoeira by the early African slaves.

Another explanation for the use of the word Capoeira is that it is closely related to the word 'capa'. A capa was a basket worn by African slaves to carry birds to the market. A 'capoeira' literally refers to the person who wears the basket. It was at the market that games of Capoeira were played, so this explanation also carries much weight. The third theory is that Capoeira finds its roots in the word 'kipura'. Kipura, meaning to flutter, is often used to describe the movements a rooster makes when he fights.

It is often said that Capoeira was developed as a form of self-defence against brutal slave masters. The musical elements are said to have been added to fool the masters into believing that the slaves were simply dancing. Evidence suggests that this account is a myth because even dancing was a forbidden practice. It can also be argued that Capoeira was no match for the guns, knives and chains used by the oppressors, and would not have been an effective form of self-defence. Capoeira in effect was an expression of African culture during a time when it faced the most oppression. Despite this suppression, Capoeira continued to flourish as an underground movement, involving secret meeting places and initiation ceremonies throughout the colonial years.

The development

In 1888, the Golden Law was passed and slavery was officially abolished in Brazil. In effect many slaves were made homeless by this and, gaining no financial assistance from the government, were forced to head to the cities in search of work. Competing for work in such a prejudiced society often proved difficult for the slaves and many turned to petty crime for survival. It was during this period that Capoeira gained its bad reputation and became associated with the criminal classes and anti-government movements. The name Capoeira became synonymous with the bandit, the thief and the vagrant. Eventually it was banned, and a Capoeirista could face the harsh punishment of having their tendons cut if they were caught playing it. Just as it had survived slavery, Capoeira continued to thrive as an outlawed practice. Capoeiristas assumed 'apelidos' (nicknames) to avoid detection from the police. This custom is still used today where Capoeiristas assume a Capoeira nickname at their first 'batizado' (baptism, or grading ceremony). This is another example of how the traditions of Capoeira derive from its ability to resist oppression.

By the twentieth century Capoeira was widespread in Brazil, but still maintained its reputation as the art of the mercenary and thief. Public opinion frowned upon it and Capoeira was driven further underground. The suppression did not abate until the 1930s, when Getulio Vargas came to power. Vargas was eager to support all forms of Brazilian cultural expression, including Capoeira. The tide was finally turning in favour of the art. It was during this time that Mestre Bimba (one of the forefathers of modern Capoeira) was invited by the State Governor General to perform an exhibition of his Capoeira Regional for foreign dignitaries. Slowly Capoeira was beginning to move away from its criminal past and towards the respectability of a martial art.

It was during the 1930s that the foundations were laid for modern Capoeira. With the permission of Getulio Vargas, Mestre Bimba opened his doors to the first Capoeira school in 1932, moving Capoeira onto a new level of organization and respectability. Mestre Bimba aimed to promote and teach Capoeira as a form of self-defence and as a disciplined martial art. He wanted to reclaim the art and free it from its criminal past. The style he developed is referred to as Capoeira Regional and is still practised as part of contemporary Capoeira. A few years later Mestre Pastinha opened an

AN EXAMPLE OF A CREATIVE ADVANCED ESCAPE BY MESTRE PONCIANINHO (IN THE AIR).

academy teaching Capoeira Angola in an effort to preserve what he saw as traditional aspects of the game, and thus the two main styles of Capoeira training were in place. Capoeira moved from being simply a spontaneous, expressive art to becoming a structured and disciplined martial art. During the 1960s and 1970s it became so structured that it was almost unrecognizable. The traditional style of Capoeira Angola began to decline, and Capoeira saw the emergence of competitions with rules and belt systems inspired by the Asian martial arts.

The history of Capoeira is still evolving. Since the 1970s, Capoeira has spread throughout Brazil and to the rest of the world. Mestres have travelled abroad and academies have opened in Europe and the USA. Despite these developments, Capoeiristas still play using the styles established by Mestre Bimba and Mestre Pastinha during the 1930s. The durability of Capoeira, its adaptability and resilience are its history. Capoeira was born from slavery and has survived oppression and globalization, enabling it to become one of the fastest growing martial arts in the world.

DEVELOPMENT

The development of contemporary Capoeira is largely indebted to the work of Mestre Bimba and Mestre Pastinha in Brazil during the 1930s. Through their work, two major styles of Capoeira were developed that are still practised within Capoeira today. Capoeira Angola is considered to be the purer form of Capoeira, having moved less from the African roots of the game. Capoeira Angola places less emphasis on acrobatic moves and high kicks, instead focusing more on 'malandragem', the guile and cunning of the game. It is considered to be a slower game than Regional and is played close to the ground. Developed by Mestre Bimba, Capoeira Regional is more widely practised in contemporary Capoeira, and is seen to place more emphasis on harder, faster moves. In contemporary Capoeira, it is vital that you have an understanding of their two distinctive styles.

Mestre Bimba and Capoeira Regional

In 1899 Manoel Dos Reis Machado was born in Salvador, Bahia. He is more commonly known as Mestre Bimba, Bimba being a nickname given to him by his mother when he was a child. He began to take informal lessons in Capoeira at the age of 12 under the instruction of an African by the name of Bentinho. He dedicated the rest of his life to Capoeira, developing a style he referred to as 'the Regional fight from Bahia'. The style and tradition is now referred to as Capoeira Regional and is practised worldwide.

When Mestre Bimba began to practise Capoeira it still had the reputation of being an art used by thieves and vagrants. Practised in the street or in workplaces, it had no organized structure and was not really considered to be a serious martial art. During the 1930s, however, Mestre Bimba set out to change this, and in 1932 he opened the first Capoeira academy. Mestre Bimba aimed to instil discipline into his students – vagrants were banned from attending classes and anyone arriving late to class was fined. Mestre Bimba famously displayed the rules of his academy on a notice board:

The nine commandments of Mestre Bimba

- Stop smoking. Smoking during training is forbidden.
- Stop drinking. Drinking affects the muscles.
- Do not use Capoeira to impress your friends. Always remember that surprise is your best friend in a fight.
- Do not talk during training. Use the time you are paying for to observe others.
- Always use the ginga.
- Practise the basic exercises daily.
- Don't be scared to get close to your opponent. You will learn more from closer play.
- Eliminate unnecessary tension from your body.
- You're better off being beaten in the roda than in the streets.

Mestre Bimba was quite an eccentric character, and the first time a student attended his academy they would be expected to undergo one of his infamous tests. Potential students were subjected to a test of physical ability, which involved being held in a neck lock by Mestre Bimba without uttering a word of complaint. On the second visit he would hold their hand and teach them the ginga (see section five, pages 34–35). He

opposite MESTRE PONCIANINHO DEMONSTRATES A 'TESOURA' (SCISSORS TAKE DOWN) WITH IMPRESSIVE PRECISION.

CAPOEIRA AT ITS BEST DEMONSTRATES ELEGANCE, STYLE AND BALANCE.

believed that the ginga was of fundamental importance within Capoeira, and that without its characteristic sway there was no Capoeira. Mestre Bimba had a hard and disciplined training style, using various techniques to toughen up his students – part of his training involved throwing stones at his students to improve their reflexes. Students were trained to fight with conviction and to leave their fear at the door. Mestre Bimba himself was a tough fighter and was often described as 'Bimba e bamba' ('Bimba is tough').

Part of the process of formalizing Capoeira was the distinction made between the beginner and the graduate. Before Mestre Bimba's era, students would pick up the moves by watching other Capoeiristas play in the street. Mestre Bimba introduced a training system that involved eight sequences of attack and defence ('sequências') and beginners were expected to perfect these before they could enter the roda. They were also expected to learn the ginga, the fundamental, basic move of Capoeira. They would go on to learn sweeping kicks and the 'cintura desprezada' (a sequence of flips culminating in the Capoeirista landing on their feet).

Mestre Bimba was an adept of Batuque – a now extinct African game that involved players attempting to knock each other down with sweeps – and Regional Capoeira's standing sweeps are formidable. He was a competitive man who wanted Capoeira to rank alongside the Asian martial arts that were being introduced into Brazil at the time. He also introduced Capoeira to the world of organized fighting, challenging other martial artists to bouts in the ring. In order to be effective against other martial arts, he introduced grappling techniques and came under heavy criticism for changing the fundamental nature of Capoeira. Mestre Bimba knew that Capoeira would have to change. He must either adapt Capoeira to the rules of the ring or move away from it, finding a new place for Capoeira that fused tradition with the fight.

Although Mestre Bimba faced criticism from some for westernizing the art, he is largely respected for helping to bring Capoeira into the modern era. By formalizing the training process and introducing uniforms and rules of conduct, he contributed to the improved image of Capoeira as an art form. Capoeira not only shed its shady image, but began to stand alongside other martial arts as a serious discipline. Although tradition was important to Mestre Bimba, he knew that by emphasizing the fighting aspect of Capoeira he would open it up to a broader audience who would not automatically relate to the traditional elements that were based in African culture. He did continue to use the music traditional to Capoeira but removed the atabaque (drum) from the bateria (orchestra) due to its connection to candonble (the religion he practised). Mestre Bimba moved Capoeira into the modern era while retaining many of the traditional elements of the art. Without this modernization, it is difficult to say whether or not Capoeira would have been lost to obscurity.

Mestre Bimba continued to practise Capoeira until his death in 1974. Even in old age, when his limbs were bent and covered in varicose veins, he could kick a younger, fitter man out of the roda. He was a strong, unbending character who moved away from his hometown of Bahia shortly before his death, feeling that the authorities had not given Capoeira the recognition it deserved. He died alone and penniless, away from the students who loved him, and gave express wishes that he would not be buried in Bahia. Throughout Brazil, academies closed their doors for seven days as a mark of respect. The respect for Mestre Bimba within the world of Capoeira continues to this day.

Mestre Pastinha and Capoeira Angola

Born in Salvador, Bahia in 1889, Vicente Ferreira Pastinha is most commonly known for preserving the style of Capoeira Angola. He was small and slight from birth and was bullied as a child. He was taken under the wing of an African named Benedito, who taught him Capoeira as a method of self-defence. Although he continued to have a slight build, Mestre Pastinha held his own against tough men, gaining a job as a bouncer in a local casino. He was also known to carry a sickle, which could be attached to his berimbau (a musical instrument), enabling it to become an offensive weapon for street fighting. Although he used Capoeira as a fighting art to defend himself on the streets, Mestre Pastinha was not simply a fighting man. He is more commonly known as the philosopher and story-teller of Capoeira, who dedicated his life to the love of the art. He loved to analyze Capoeira, to muse on its meanings and moves, and was the first popular Capoeirista to write a book on the subject.

Although many Capoeira Mestres respected the work of Mestre Bimba, others were opposed to the extent to which Capoeira had been modernized. Many resisted the changes made and looked back towards the origins of Capoeira, its African roots. Mestre Pastinha opened his academy a few years after Mestre Bimba and sought to teach what he believed to be a purer form of Capoeira. This form of Capoeira became known as 'Capoeira Angola'. The name Angola makes reference to the African slaves who first practised the art, many of whom originated from Angola.

Like Mestre Bimba, Mestre Pastinha saw Capoeira as a discipline and tried to distinguish it from the violent forms of Capoeira played on the street. He also wanted to improve the image of Capoeira, and by moving it away from the streets and in to the academy he could provide some discipline. By adding a level of hierarchy and structure, he aimed to stop the use of violent and uncontrolled conduct. He placed great emphasis on the role of the mestre within the roda, believing that it was his duty to keep control. He also believed that his role of mestre gave him the responsibility to ensure that the traditions were continued. He aimed to keep Capoeira pure. Moves from other martial arts were banned, as were high kicks and any form of grappling. He also placed much emphasis on the music of Capoeira, composing many of his own rhythms and songs. Mestre Pastinha recognized the beauty and elegance the music added to the art, and even today you will not see Capoeira Angola played without the music. Mestre Pastinha also introduced uniforms to his academy. The colours black and yellow were taken from his favourite football team, Ipiranga, and are still used by many Angoleiros today.

Mestre Pastinha understood the fighting nature of Capoeira, but firmly believed that it could never be purely competitive. He placed much emphasis on the process and nature of the game and not on winning and losing. He promoted fair play, manners and loyalty, placing great emphasis on the 'jogo de dentro' (the 'inner game'). The inner game is essential to Capoeira Angola, demonstrating the students' guile, cunning and inner strength. Mestre Pastinha took a holistic approach to Capoeira, believing that a student's development could be more than just physical. He acknowledged the psychological and spiritual aspects of Capoeira and believed that it could be of benefit to all. He is most famously quoted as saying 'Capoeira is for men, women and children. The only ones who don't learn Capoeira are those who don't wish to'.

Mestre Pastinha's approach to Capoeira attracted the attention of intellectuals and artists, many of whom became his friends. These connections helped him to open a school in a colonial building, establishing himself as the principal Angoleiro of his day. So successful was Mestre Pastinha's Capoeira Angola that in the 1960s, tourists visited his academy to witness displays of 'authentic Capoeira'. In the 1970s, however, his fortunes took a turn for the worse. His academy was repossessed by the Foundation for Artistic and Cultural Heritage and was never returned. He lost all of his possessions and even though he opened another academy it never matched the scale and prestige of his former years. Mestre Pastinha eventually lost his eyesight and died penniless in an institution for the elderly. Like Mestre Bimba, he felt let down by the authorities.

It was assumed after his death that Capoeira Angola would fade into obscurity, being eclipsed by the more dynamic style of Regional and seen simply as a dying art for old men. With the growing success of the Regional schools in Rio, it would appear that Angola had seen better days and that the traditions it embraced were being pushed aside. During the 1980s, however, there was a renewed interest in Afro-Brazilian culture, leading to an increased interest in Capoeira Angola. As the Angola style was perceived to be a purer form of Capoeira, it was thought to embody more of the traditions passed down from its African originators. In order to revive the dying art, the Grupo

CAPOEIRA IS RAPIDLY GROWING IN POPULARITY. IT IS TAUGHT IN GYMS, DANCE STUDIOS, UNIVERSITIES AND SCHOOLS ACROSS THE WORLD.

de Capoeira Angola Pelourinho was formed. They called old Capoeira Angola mestres out of obscurity to train with them and, in defiance of the faster, acrobatic forms of the art, encouraged younger men to practise Capoeira Angola. It ceased to be an old man's game, with younger Capoeiristas, such as Mestre Cobra Mansa, proving that it could be just as efficient a fighting technique as the Regional style.

Cordão de Ouro

Since Mestre Bimba and Mestre Pastinha opened their academies in the 1930s, countless groups have developed throughout the world. One of these is the school I belong to, Cordão de Ouro ('Golden Belt'). Cordão de Ouro was formed in 1967 by Mestre Brasilia and Grand Mestre Suassuna. Mestre Reinaldo Ramos Suassuna was born in Itabuna, Bahia in 1942. He began Capoeira following doctor's orders to improve the health of his joints. He was not a natural Capoeirista and found the ginga difficult to master. After years of dedicated training he became a mestre in Capoeira and developed a new style called Miudinho. He felt that there was something missing in Capoeira, that the game lacked a closeness and that Capoeiristas were playing too far away from each other. When he watched the games of mestres such as Mestre Joao Grande and Mestre Joao Pequeno, who played the jogo de dentro, he feared the style would be lost to younger generations. He developed the Miudinho style in order to revive the inner game, common in Capoeira Angola. The word miudinho quite literally means 'smaller', and Mestre Suassuna could often be heard instructing his students to 'play smaller' and to 'get closer'. Many of his training techniques were developed to help his students play together more closely. He would place a berimbau (a monochordic musical instrument) across two chairs and ask his students to play Capoeira underneath it, almost in a limbo fashion. They had no choice but to play a lower game. Mestre Suassuna also admired the expressive moves of the old Capoeiristas and developed ways of training students in the expressive aspect of Capoeira. He added ornamental aspects to the ginga, making it more dance-like, and encouraged students to mimic animals in order to find new ways of expression within their game. Mestre Suassuna also composed variations of the 'toques' (rhythms) played on the berimbau. One toque instructed the players to bring the level of the game up and to use higher movements. Another toque was used to call the players back to the foot of the berimbau if a game was not proceeding well. Mestre Suassuna was conscious of the need to appeal to young people, so he created challenging moves such as back bends and twists. He incorporated these moves into the game so that they were not simply an exhibition of acrobatics. Through the hard work and dedication of its founding members, Cordão de Ouro went on to become one of the most successful schools in São Paulo.

A family affair

My own mestre is my father, Jose Antonio dos Santos de Almeida, a student of Mestre Suassuna. He was born in Brazil in 1958 and is mestre of Cordão de Ouro in my home town of Guaratinguetá, São Paulo. He has been teaching Capoeira for 25 years. Through Capoeira he also works with homeless children, helping them to improve the quality of their lives. Mestre Antonio supervises Cordão de Ouro in London (where I am currently mestre under the name of Poncianinho – 'Little Ponciano') and he visits England several times a year to teach workshops and to supervise 'batizados' (grading ceremonies). I was born in Guaratinguetá in 1980 and began playing Capoeira at just four years old. I took to it like a duck to water, and by the age of 15 I was teaching within the group. Cordão de Ouro respect and value the traditions and styles of the past, and we study and preserve the roots of both Capoeira Angola and Capoeira Regional.

A YOUNG PONCIANO SHOWS THAT EXCELLENT FLEXIBILITY IS VITAL.

Contemporary Capoeira

In 1972 Capoeira was officially recognized in Brazil as an official sport, and by the 1980s it had spread from Bahia, Rio de Janeiro and São Paulo to the whole of Brazil. By the 1990s Capoeira was being taught on all the continents of the world, and was represented in every state in the USA. It is estimated that several million people play Capoeira worldwide. Capoeiristas come from all ethnic backgrounds, socio-economic groups and genders. Women now make up a substantial number of students, fulfilling Mestre Pastinha's wish that Capoeira was for all who were willing to learn the art.

Contemporary Capoeira can no longer simply be split into Angola and Regional styles, with many groups using elements of both styles to teach their students. Although there are core moves and traditions within Capoeira, the style can vary from group to group, making contemporary Capoeira a rich and varied art.

WITH THE RIGHT ATTITUDE AND THE RIGHT TEACHER, CAPOEIRA STUDENTS CAN DEVELOP FANTASTIC SKILLS IN JUST A FEW YEARS.

TRAINING

It is very important to take a serious approach during training to ensure safety. Your spatial awareness will improve in time, but it is important to try to be aware of the existence of others around you. Capoeira is a very safe sport, but you should be aware that most accidents happen while training and not while playing or fighting. Accidents and injuries tend to happen when students are not aware of the speed and the correct position of the foot while kicking, or are not paying due attention while attacking. Extra care must be taken when practising spinning kicks, the aú (cartwheel) and other tumbling movements.

Approach to training

Positive thinking is essential during training, as you will not perform well in every class – often finding the movements and correct technique difficult to master. Persistence is the key. Never allow your frustration to get the better of you. For the more experienced Capoeirista there are different phases in your Capoeira training, and you may face times where you feel that you are making slow or very minimal progress, whether in your technique or in your game. There are many challenges within Capoeira with so many things to learn. When you get to a certain level you will notice more movements within the game, but you may not have reached the level of flexibility or strength to reproduce these movements. At this stage you might begin to put more pressure on yourself and have higher expectations, but it is better to have a clear understanding of the moves and approach them step by step. Each mestre will have their own way of teaching, and systems within each group may vary. By paying close attention to your particular mestre your game will improve immensely. It is also important to share the knowledge you gain within Capoeira, as this will develop your future ability to teach and to clarify in your own mind the moves your body makes. A student that never shares may become an egotistical Capoeirista who will never reach his full potential.

No one approach will enable you to achieve your goals, as Capoeira is a holistic art. I believe that only a combination of elements can lead to progress, and my mestre taught me three basic rules of training:

Three basic rules of training

- Quality in the technique and appropriate amount of training.
- Good nutrition.
- Rest.

Combining a good amount of training hours with a balanced diet and sufficient rest will make a considerable difference to your performance.

The mind will also play an important role in your performance, skill and ability to succeed in Capoeira. Capoeira can help you to be a more positive and energetic person, but you must be strong at difficult moments and show strength of character. The way you live your life outside of the class, in your daily life and on the streets, will reflect in your game. Be aware of your fears and insecurities and be careful that they don't transform into submission or aggression. Capoeira is the art of being able to fight with a smile on your face.

opposite MANY FACTORS COMBINE TO MAKE A GOOD CAPOEIRISTA, BUT GOOD NUTRITION, REST AND TRAINING ARE THE BASICS.

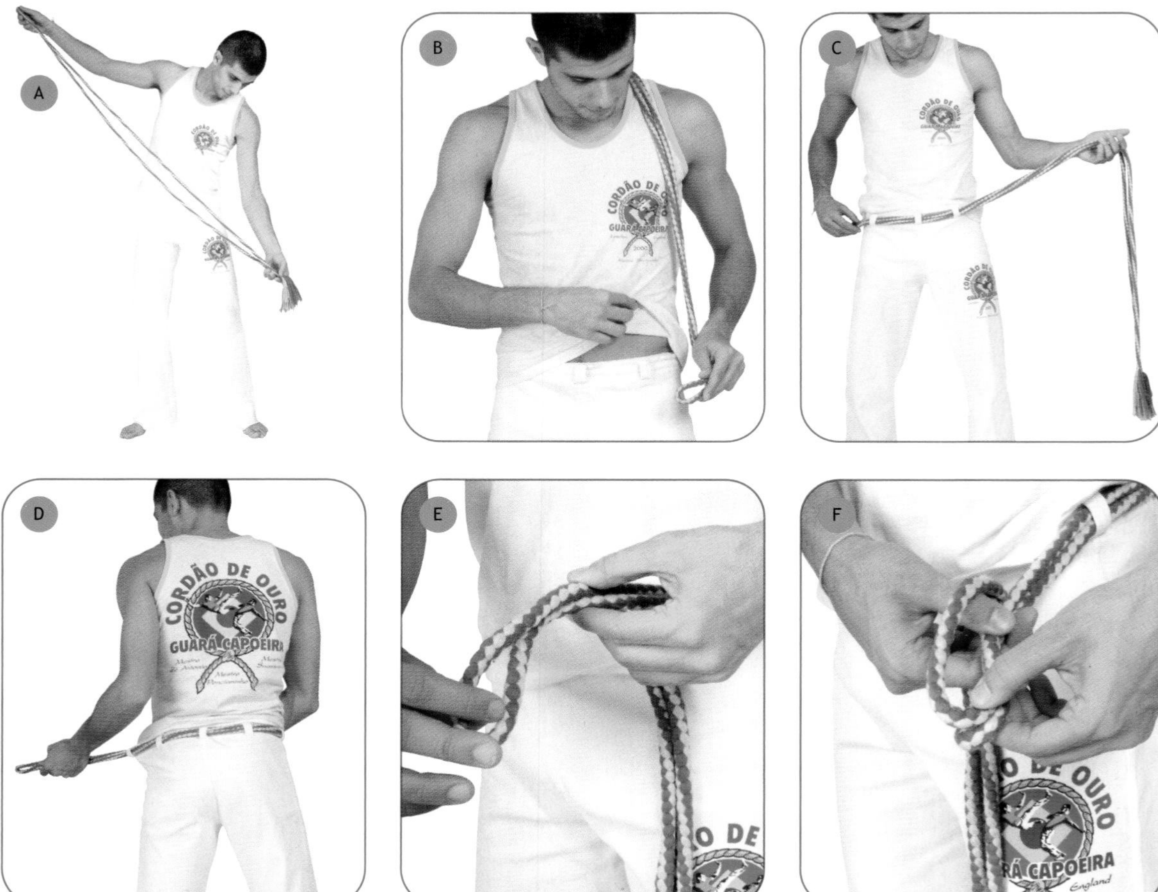

How to tie the Capoeira belt

The Capoeira belt is called the 'cordão' (cord). Some groups may call their belt the 'corda' (rope), depending on how it is made. There are a few different types of belts in Capoeira, and the Capoeira cordão differs from belts in other martial arts because it is a cord shape and not flat. The cordão is made from wool and is woven with the colour, or colours, of the grade. The corda is a rope that is dyed to the colour of each grade. My own group, Cordão de Ouro, uses cordãos that are woven in the traditional way by the students of the academy in the lead up to the batizado. The weaving of the belts is time-consuming, so some groups buy the belts pre-woven. All of the belts for my London group are hand-woven by students of my father's academy in Brazil.

A Double up your belt, making sure the ends are at equal lengths.

B Feed the middle part of your belt through the first belt loop to the left of your Capoeira trousers.

C Take the belt through the first three belt loops.

D Continue to feed the belt through all of the belt loops.

E Once your belt has been fed through the last belt loop and is back round to your left side, take the end of the belt in your right hand.

F Fold the belt back and put your fingers through the loop to hold the lower part of the belt, which you can see through the loop that has just been made.

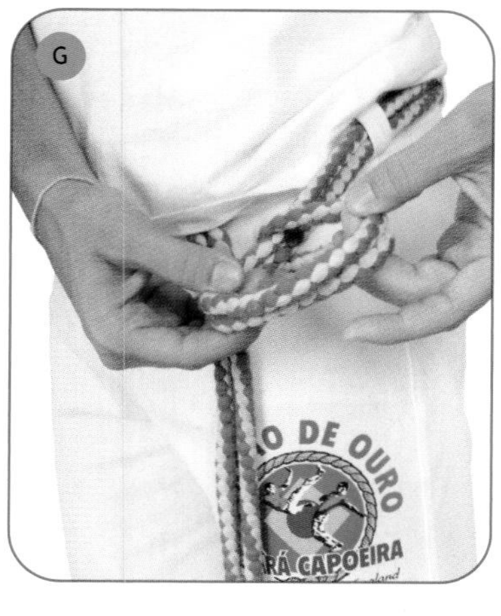

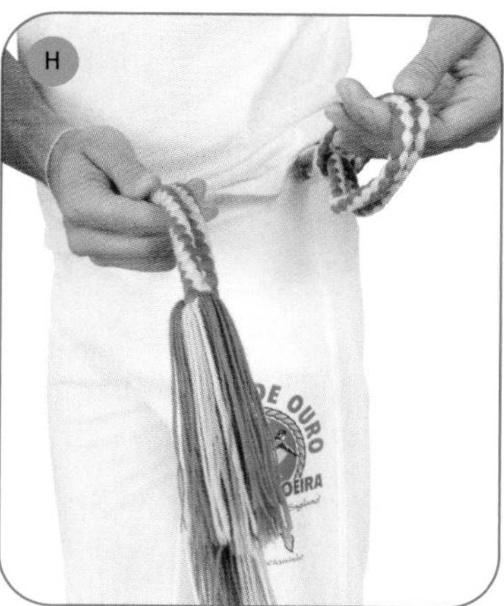

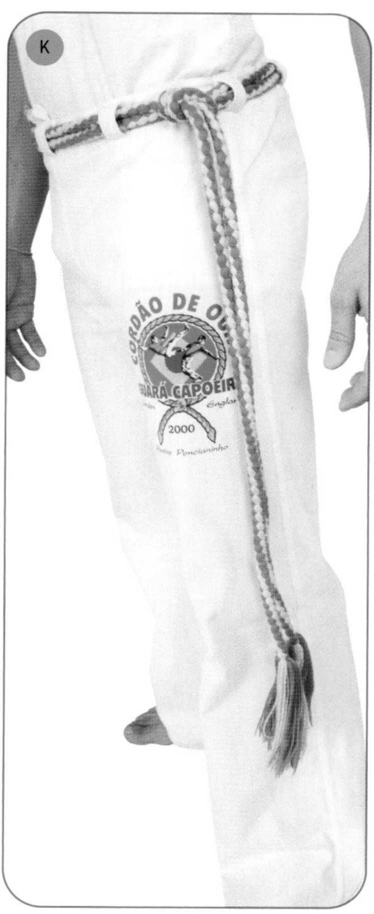

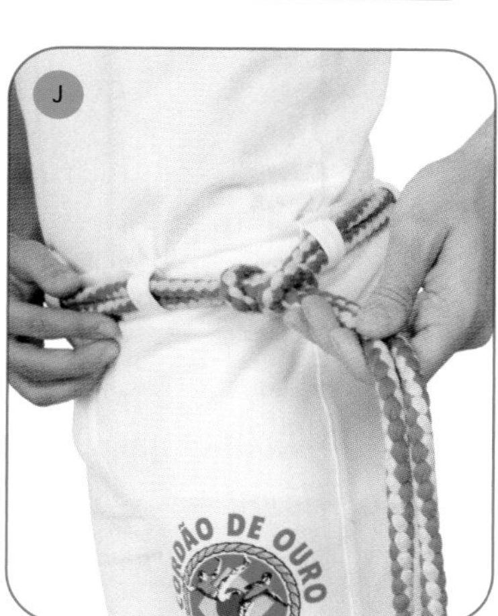

G Pull the doubled up part of the belt you have just taken with your right hand and take it through the top end of the belt that you had first folded back, in order to create a new loop. Hold the new loop in your left hand.

H Take hold of the other end of the belt, holding the loop open with your right hand.

I Feed the ends of your belt through the loop and pull it through.

J Pull the end of your belt tight.

K A correctly tied belt will stay tied while you are practising and playing Capoeira, and will also be easy to untie.

Uniforms

Most groups wear white uniforms consisting of trousers and a t-shirt or vest. The white uniform comes from an old tradition where the Capoeiristas would play wearing white suits – a highly skilled player would emerge from the game with an unmarked suit. The group logo is normally emblazoned on the front of the uniform. Capoeira trousers are made of fabric that stretches to allow maximum movement.

Warming up

The warm-up is the first part of any Capoeira class and should be taken as seriously as the actual learning of the movements. The warm-up raises the body temperature and improves the oxygen supply to the muscles. This stimulates blood sugar and adrenaline levels, preparing the body for action. The preparation of the heart muscle for rigorous exercise is particularly important to individuals who have cardiovascular problems. Warm-up reduces the workload on the cardiac muscle and helps to provide it with an adequate blood supply. Always talk to your doctor, though, before beginning any exercise regime. The warm-up also prepares your body for the stress of activity and will help to improve your performance. It also helps to prevent or reduce muscle soreness, strains, and the tearing of muscle fibres or tendons.

The basic moves of Capoeira can also be used in the warm-up section. It is very important for your joints to be warmed up thoroughly to prepare your body for the impact of kicks, falls and the hyper-extended movements that they will endure. A Capoeira warm-up begins with small movements to mobilize your joints. These will be incorporated into base moves such as the ginga and cocorinha to a relatively slow rhythm, and will usually run straight through to the first part of your technical training. A safe and efficient warm-up should have a gradual build of intensity and last no less than ten minutes. It is always a good idea for you to arrive early and find a space for you to start warming up before the class – this way you will gain more from your training.

D

E

F

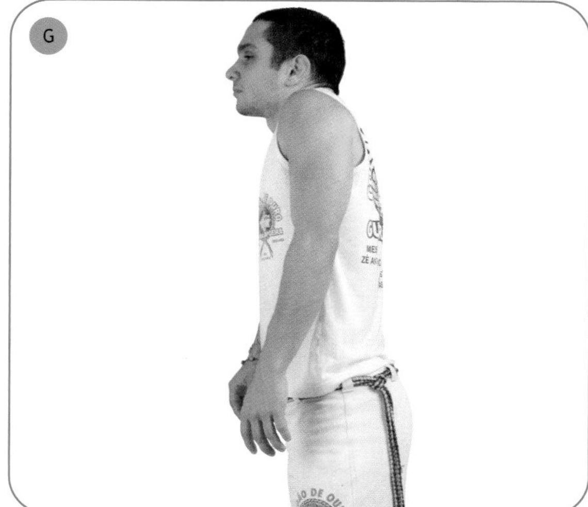

G

Mobilizing the neck and shoulders

A Start in a relaxed position facing the front with your feet shoulder-width apart and your knees soft.

B—C Look to the left and right over your shoulders, keeping the abdominals firm and the spine long. Repeat this several times.

D—E Maintain the same posture and bring your ear towards your shoulder to the right and left. Gently stretch the side of your neck and keep the spine long as you go through the central position of the head.

F—G—H From a standing position, bring your shoulders forward and up towards your ears and back round in a clockwise motion, creating circular movements with both shoulders.

(Continued)

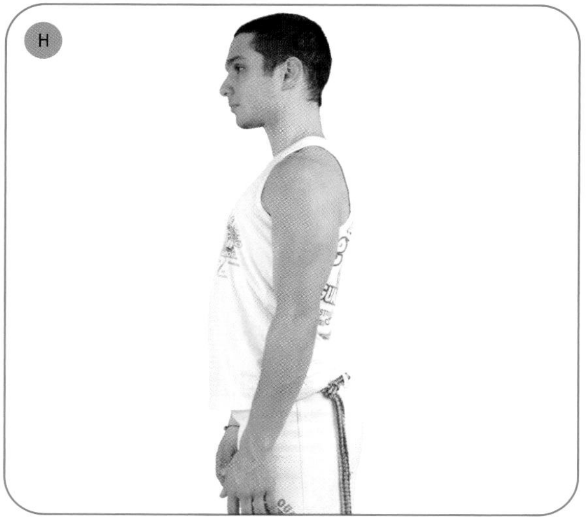

H

(Continued)

I Start from a standing position with your abdominals firm, facing forward.

J Bring your head and shoulders forward and start to roll down through your spine towards the floor.

K Roll through your spine all the way down to the floor and let your upper body hang over.

L Roll back up through your spine leaving your head relaxed forward.

M Return to an upright standing position and repeat the exercise several times.

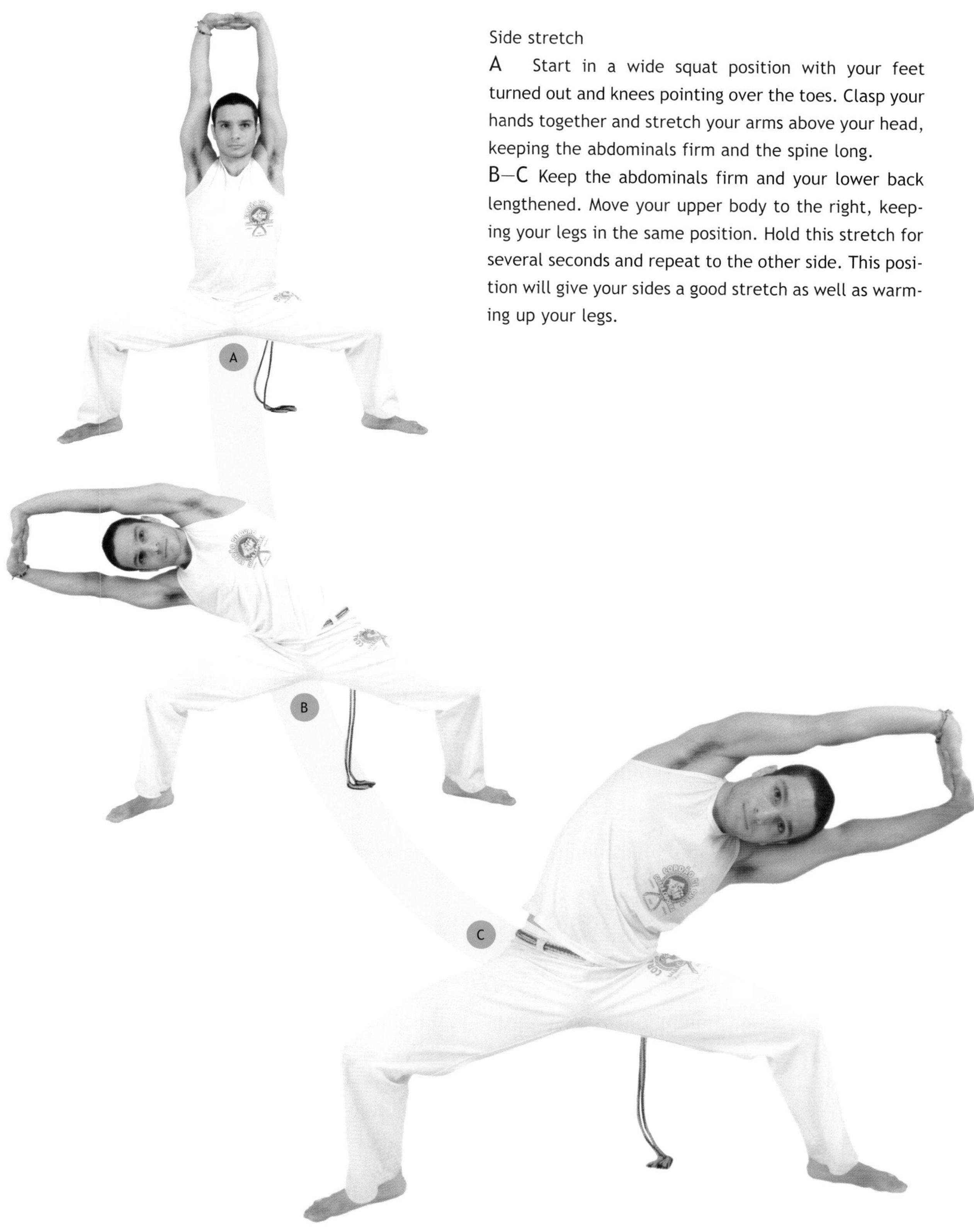

Side stretch

A Start in a wide squat position with your feet turned out and knees pointing over the toes. Clasp your hands together and stretch your arms above your head, keeping the abdominals firm and the spine long.

B—C Keep the abdominals firm and your lower back lengthened. Move your upper body to the right, keeping your legs in the same position. Hold this stretch for several seconds and repeat to the other side. This position will give your sides a good stretch as well as warming up your legs.

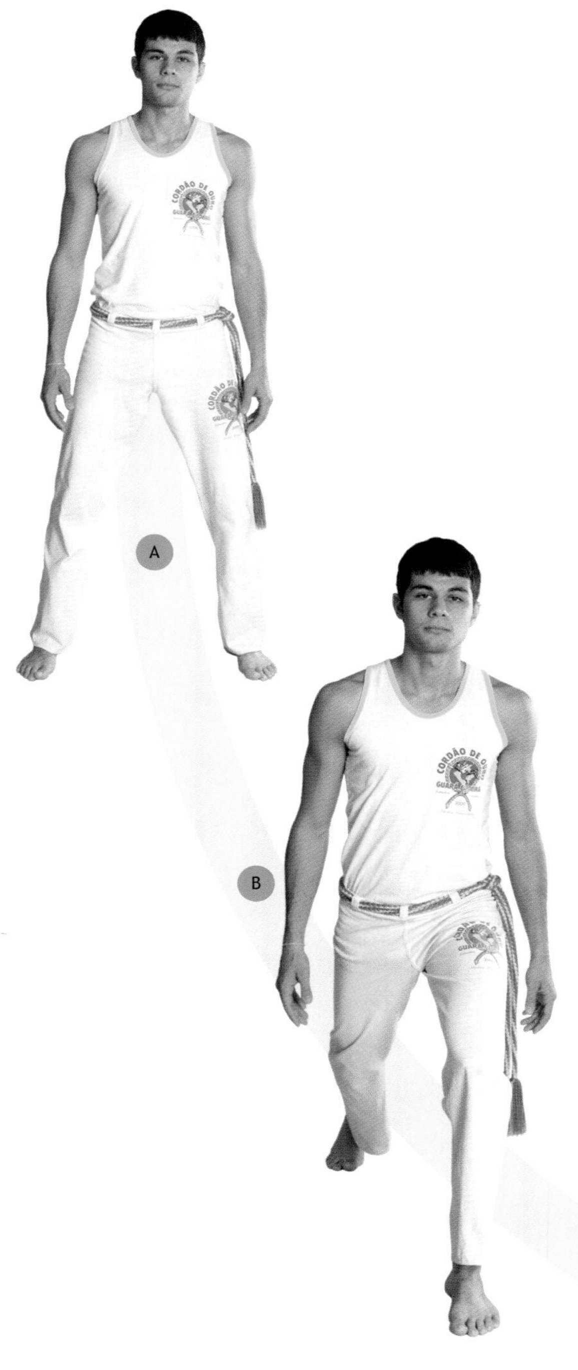

The ginga

The ginga (pronounced 'jinga') is fundamental to Capoeira and is the first movement you should learn. It is the ginga that creates the natural swing or sway, and combined with the music makes Capoeira a unique martial art. Its use is vital within Capoeira, as it helps you to develop spatial awareness and a keen sense of rhythm. Many movements derive from the ginga and it should never be neglected within your game.

The ginga is an important part of your training and you will usually start to ginga as part of your warm-up, gradually incorporating other moves as you progress. You can use the ginga within the game to escape, attack, counter-attack, and confuse your opponent. Your aim is to develop a strong base in your ginga and work towards achieving your own natural swing or

B (SIDEVIEW)

sway; this will help you to develop expression within your game. Each Capoeirista will have their own style of ginga, and it is important to try to find your own way of expressing yourself through this basic movement. When you begin to practise with the music, you will start to connect your body to the rhythms that are being played by the bateria, and this will allow you to feel the swing of the ginga.

The ginga will enable you to move around the roda. This is the movement used to change direction within the game, according to the position of your opponent. The speed and style of the ginga will depend on the nature of the game – the ginga may be fast or slow, sharp or smooth.

A Stand with your feet parallel and shoulder-width apart. Look straight ahead, keeping your knees soft, and maintain a strong sense of grounding.

B The ginga starts by bringing your right foot backwards, touching the floor with the ball of your foot. Bring the same foot back to the initial position (picture A) and repeat with the left leg, making a triangle shape on the floor. Repeat with each leg in a continual motion. Note: Your hips must be facing forward the whole time.

C As you bring the right leg backwards, bring the right arm forward and across your chest, leaving the left arm out to the side. Repeat this movement with the left leg and combine them to produce a simultaneous movement. You will switch the arms as you switch the legs simultaneously.

C

C (SIDEVIEW)

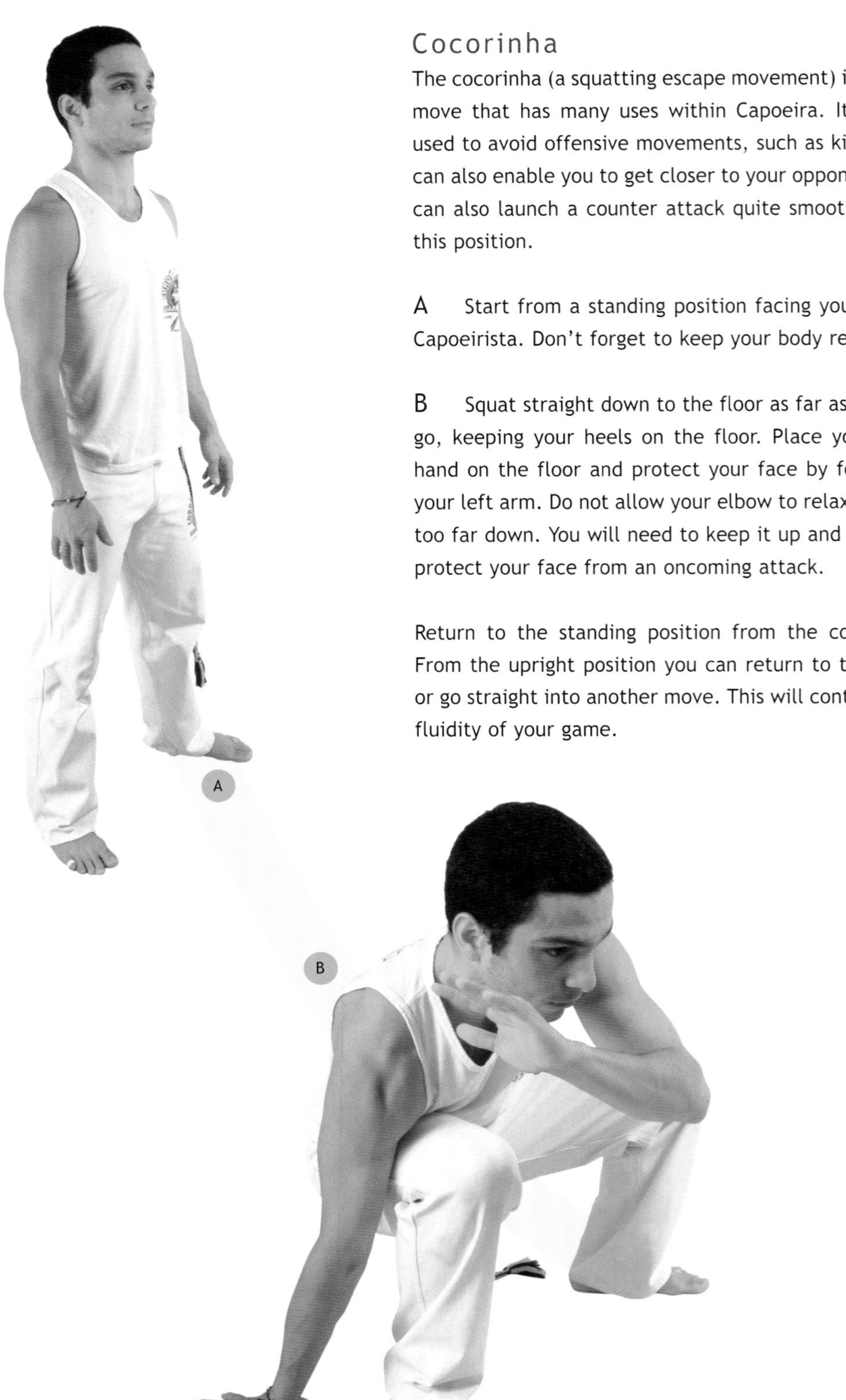

Cocorinha

The cocorinha (a squatting escape movement) is a basic move that has many uses within Capoeira. It can be used to avoid offensive movements, such as kicks, and can also enable you to get closer to your opponent. You can also launch a counter attack quite smoothly from this position.

A Start from a standing position facing your fellow Capoeirista. Don't forget to keep your body relaxed.

B Squat straight down to the floor as far as you can go, keeping your heels on the floor. Place your right hand on the floor and protect your face by folding in your left arm. Do not allow your elbow to relax and fall too far down. You will need to keep it up and ready to protect your face from an oncoming attack.

Return to the standing position from the cocorinha. From the upright position you can return to the ginga or go straight into another move. This will continue the fluidity of your game.

Queda de rins

'Queda de rins' quite literally means a fall onto the kidneys. It's a grounded movement that brings you close to the floor. Your body is lowered onto your elbow, which is locked into the side of your body just around the hip. Queda de rins is another classic Capoeira move that clearly differentiates Capoeira from other martial arts. This movement can be used to defend yourself when the knees are brought in close to your body. The queda de rins technique can also be used during a kick, such as a meia lua de compasso, thus lowering the level of the kick.

The queda de rins increases upper body strength tremendously, and it will also increase your agility and help you to gain more body control. The use of this technique, once perfected, can be useful in many moves and situations to balance and turn. There are many varieties of fall that stem from the basic queda de rins, and highly skilled movements using it can be found frequently in a game of miudinho. This technique can be used to balance and hold a position, or can be used as a transition from one move to another.

A We have shown this movement from the back to give you a clear idea of where exactly you need to lock your elbow into the side. Start from a small squat position facing the front.

B Shift your body weight to the right by placing your right hand on the floor. Bring your left arm up over your head and keep your focus forward.

C Bring the left arm up all the way over your head and place it on the floor. Coming up off of your heels, push your body weight into the right foot.

(Continued)

D

E

F

(Continued)

D Lower your body to the right elbow, with the side of your head resting on the floor and your left arm placed in front of your body for support. In this example the right knee is resting slightly on the floor with the left leg extended out. Normally the right knee should not touch the floor, but as a beginner you can put your knee on the floor until you are strong enough to maintain the position sufficiently to raise it.

E Stay in the same position and bring your knees in towards your chest. Notice how your elbow is locked into the left side just above your hip

F Aim to balance with your elbow locked into your side and keep your knees tucked in towards your chest. Use your left hand on the floor in front of you to support your balance.

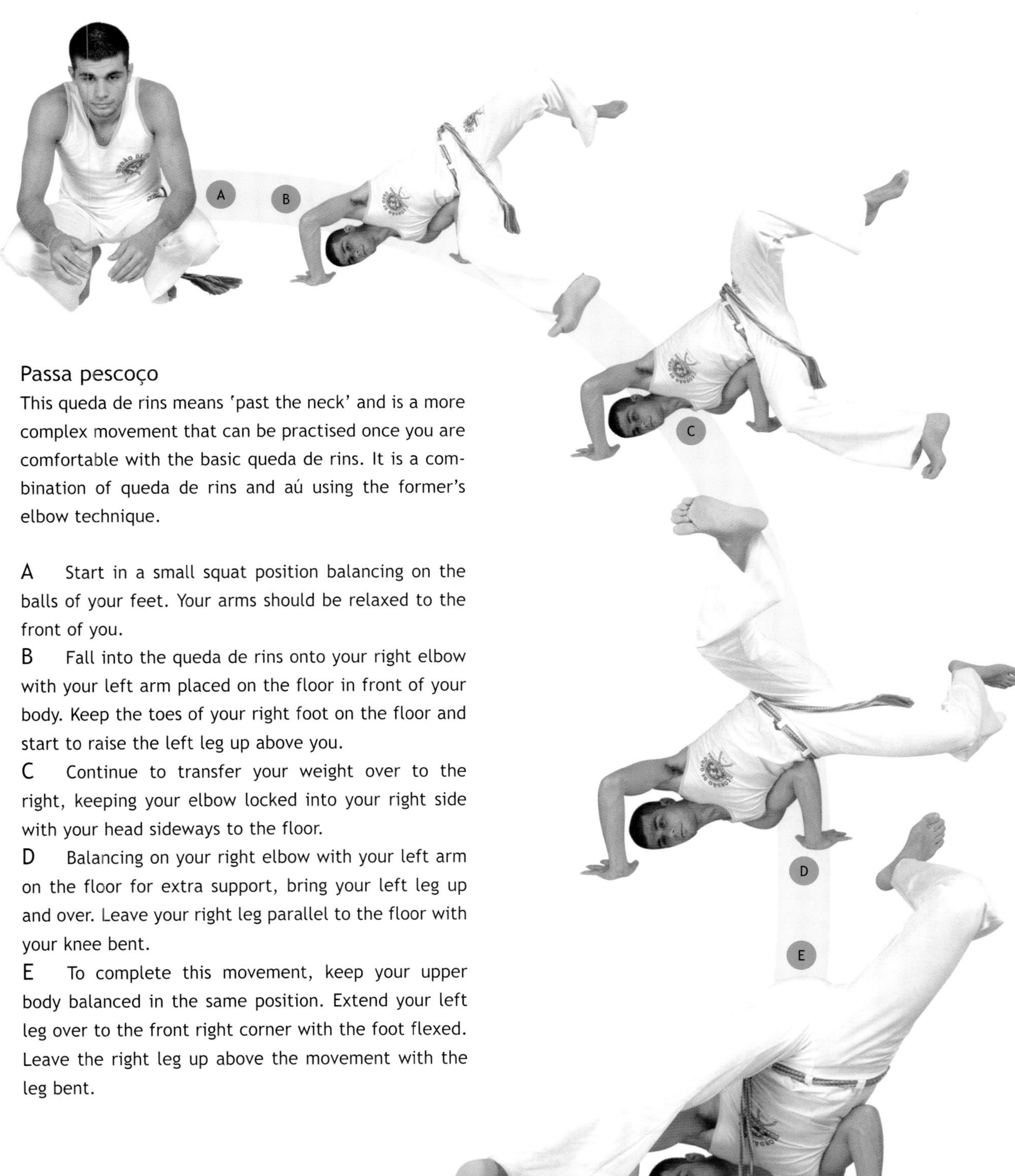

Passa pescoço

This queda de rins means 'past the neck' and is a more complex movement that can be practised once you are comfortable with the basic queda de rins. It is a combination of queda de rins and aú using the former's elbow technique.

A Start in a small squat position balancing on the balls of your feet. Your arms should be relaxed to the front of you.

B Fall into the queda de rins onto your right elbow with your left arm placed on the floor in front of your body. Keep the toes of your right foot on the floor and start to raise the left leg up above you.

C Continue to transfer your weight over to the right, keeping your elbow locked into your right side with your head sideways to the floor.

D Balancing on your right elbow with your left arm on the floor for extra support, bring your left leg up and over. Leave your right leg parallel to the floor with your knee bent.

E To complete this movement, keep your upper body balanced in the same position. Extend your left leg over to the front right corner with the foot flexed. Leave the right leg up above the movement with the leg bent.

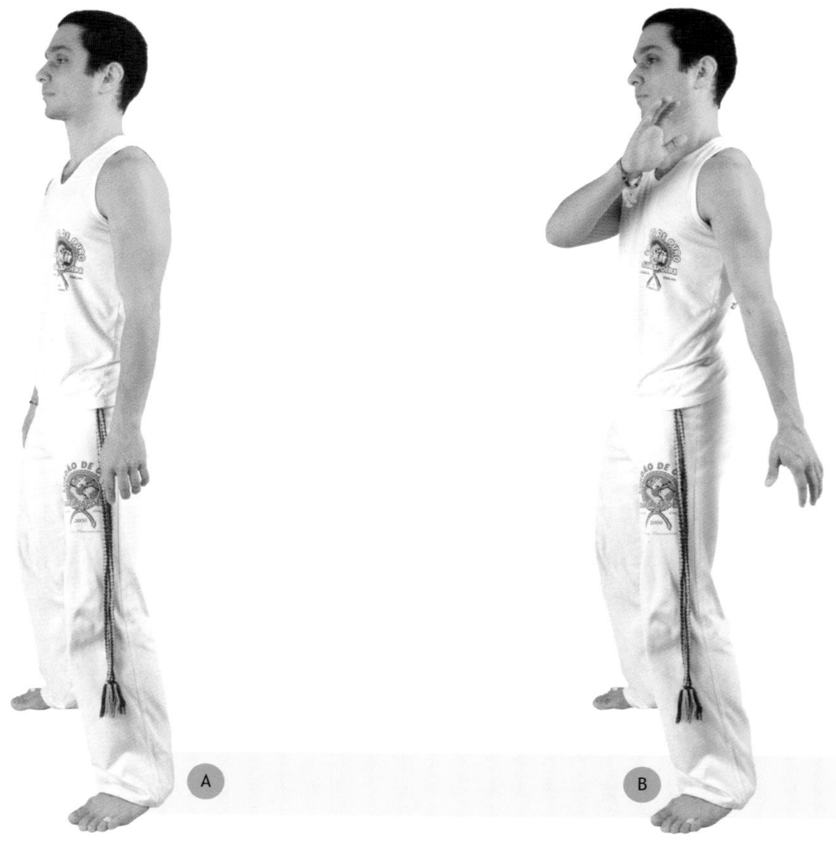

Defence and escape moves

Resistência

Resistência ('to resist') is a classic Capoeira move and an ideal movement for beginners. It will help to strengthen your back and begin to give you an understanding of arching backwards. This movement is also an effective defence movement and is the root of many advanced escapes. In training for it, you will also improve the flexibility of your lower back.

A Start from a relaxed standing position.

B Bring your right arm up and across to protect your face and allow your left arm to swing back slightly behind your body.

C As your knees bend, arch your lower back and push your pelvis forward. Your left arm continues to swing back and your right arm comes up higher to protect your face, with the elbow ready to angle itself higher if it is necessary to protect the face further.

D The resistência can go as far back as necessary; however it is important for you to prevent your head from tilting back, as eye contact needs to be maintained with your fellow Capoeirista.

E You can practise this move alone to gain strength in the lower back and also with a fellow Capoeirista to improve your reflex. This move can be practised with a few different kicks – here we have used a benção. Notice how the resistência is allowing the Capoeirista to escape the kick while maintaining eye contact. From this position the Capoeirista executing the resistência could attempt to transform the resistência into a disiqulibrante, such as a rasteira, to take his fellow Capoeirista off balance.

C
D
E

Esquiva

Esquiva is a basic movement that is used to escape from kicks. The term means 'to dodge', which is the basic purpose of the movement. There are a few variations of this movement to enable you to adapt your escape, depending on which angle an attack is coming from and on the next movement you intend to execute. In order to connect the esquiva to other moves or directions, it is important to know the various types of esquivas. The general rule of any type of esquiva is that one leg takes the majority of your body weight and that you are using your arms correctly to enable you to protect your face and upper body.

Esquiva baixa (low escape)

A Start from the ginga position and make sure that you have a good solid base with depth. Keep your right arm up to protect your face and maintain a forward focus.

B Slide your right foot back, allowing the ginga position to become wider and deeper. As you do this your hand reaches for the floor to support your balance, your chest moves towards your left thigh and your right arm comes up to protect your face. You should feel well balanced, grounded and strong in this position. Don't forget to maintain eye contact all the way through. To return from this movement you can either return to a ginga position or connect the esquiva baixa to a low floor movement.

C Here the esquiva baixa is being used to escape a meia lua de compasso. The Capoeirista in the esquiva baixa has a good, strong, balanced base that will allow her to move to any position she chooses at ease, whether it be an upright or low move.

Esquiva lateral (sideways escape)

A Start from the ginga position with your right leg back.

B Step sideways with your right leg so that you move into a lunge position. Your right foot should be turned out and your right knee bent. Your left foot stays parallel with the leg straight, the weight of the body needs to be mainly on your right leg.

C Lower your chest to your right knee and bring your right arm behind your leg with your hand on the floor. Fold your left arm in to protect your face.

From the esqiva position come straight back up to the ginga position and continue to ginga. You can then repeat this on the other side starting from the ginga position. Repeating this movement to Capoeira music will create a 'swing'.

To come out of the esquiva baixa you return to a parallel position ready to practise this movement with the other leg. Always practise on both sides, as you never know which side your opponent's attack may come from. In a class situation we would practise this move both alone and with a partner. As a beginner, start slowly with a partner and very gradually increase the speed. Take care not to anticipate the esquiva before the attack, as the main point of the exercise is to train your reflexes and not simply to practise the move.

Negativa

The direct translation of negativa is 'negative', but the actual significance of this word in relation to its purpose would be 'to reject' – you would be refusing an attack by allowing it to go over your body. The negativa is a very dynamic movement that enables you to move in different directions and to escape at the same time. It is a basic movement that teaches you to move on the floor. Many floor movements start from this move – not only can you protect yourself with the negativa, but you can also increase the fluidity within your game with the use of this movement. Once you have learnt the negativa, try to link it to other moves, such as aú de cabeça, in order to make your game more interesting. There are a few types of negativa that use the same name, but differ in form and purpose.

Negativa 1

This type of negativa can be found in most of Mestre Bimba's Regional-style sequences.

A Start from the ginga position, with the left foot forward and the right foot back. Your right arm should be up to protect your face with the left arm down to your left side.

B Bring the back leg from the ginga position through by swinging your leg forward. Keep your leg turned out, with your foot flexed and your toes pointed forward. At the same time move both your arms to your right side over your right leg. Bend the left knee, allowing you to carry yourself to the floor. Your arms need to be well over to enable you to land on the floor before any other part of your body touches the ground.

C As your hands reach the floor, your foot is kept off the ground and should be flexed with your toes pointing towards the right. Your head is positioned so that your ear is parallel to the floor – this way you can maintain your focus to the front.

D This is the full negativa position. Notice how the Capoeirista is using her strength to keep her body off the floor. Do not allow your body to collapse or your leg to rest on the floor. Your arms need to be ready to spring your body back into action. Your right elbow is kept close to your right side and your left hand should be in a good position, enabling you to support your body comfortably.

E Here you can see the negativa in action. The Capoeirista has lowered herself down with speed and efficiency to hook her right foot around the base leg of her fellow Capoeirsta's benção kick. This enables her to test his balance if desired.

C
D
E

To return from this full negativa position you can use the following saida (exit).

A Push your hands into the floor, bringing your body up. Maintain the negativa position, but allow your arms to stretch and your right foot to rest on the floor.

B Using your hands and the right foot that has just been placed on the floor, bring your body around and slightly rise onto your right foot bringing your left heel towards your backside.

C Place your left foot onto the floor until you are in a lunge position with your hands on the floor, and look through your arms and legs at your partner.

D Return to an upright position by coming up and swivelling your feet and body round to face your partner in the ginga position, with your right leg back.

Negativa 2

The following negativa is more commonly found in a game of Capoeira Angola. This movement can be executed from a ginga position. It is a low escape and once well-trained you can move from this position into any other movement with speed and ease for an effective escape. This negativa can also be used as a fall. If your opponent attacks you with a sweep it is an excellent position to fall into, as you can land in a well-balanced position, enabling you to make a quick recovery into another movement.

A Start in a squat position, with your heels slightly raised off the floor. Your weight should be on the balls of your feet and you should have a good, balanced position.

B Move your body to the side. Place both of your hands on the floor to the side of your body. Stretch your left leg out to the side with your right knee pointing forward. Your right heel remains off the floor.

(Continued)

(Continued)

C Lower your body to the side to the full negativa position. Your head stays parallel to the floor enabling you to maintain a forward focus and your right elbow comes in close to the right side of your body. In this position you are taking the full weight of your body on your arms, preventing your body from collapsing on to the floor.

D To come out of the negativa, push up your body with your arms, keeping the right heel off the floor.

E Bring your right arm over your head as you swivel your body to the left using your right foot and your left arm. Continue to maintain eye contact with your partner.

F Continue to swivel your body on your left foot and place your free hand on the floor. Start to bring your right leg around.

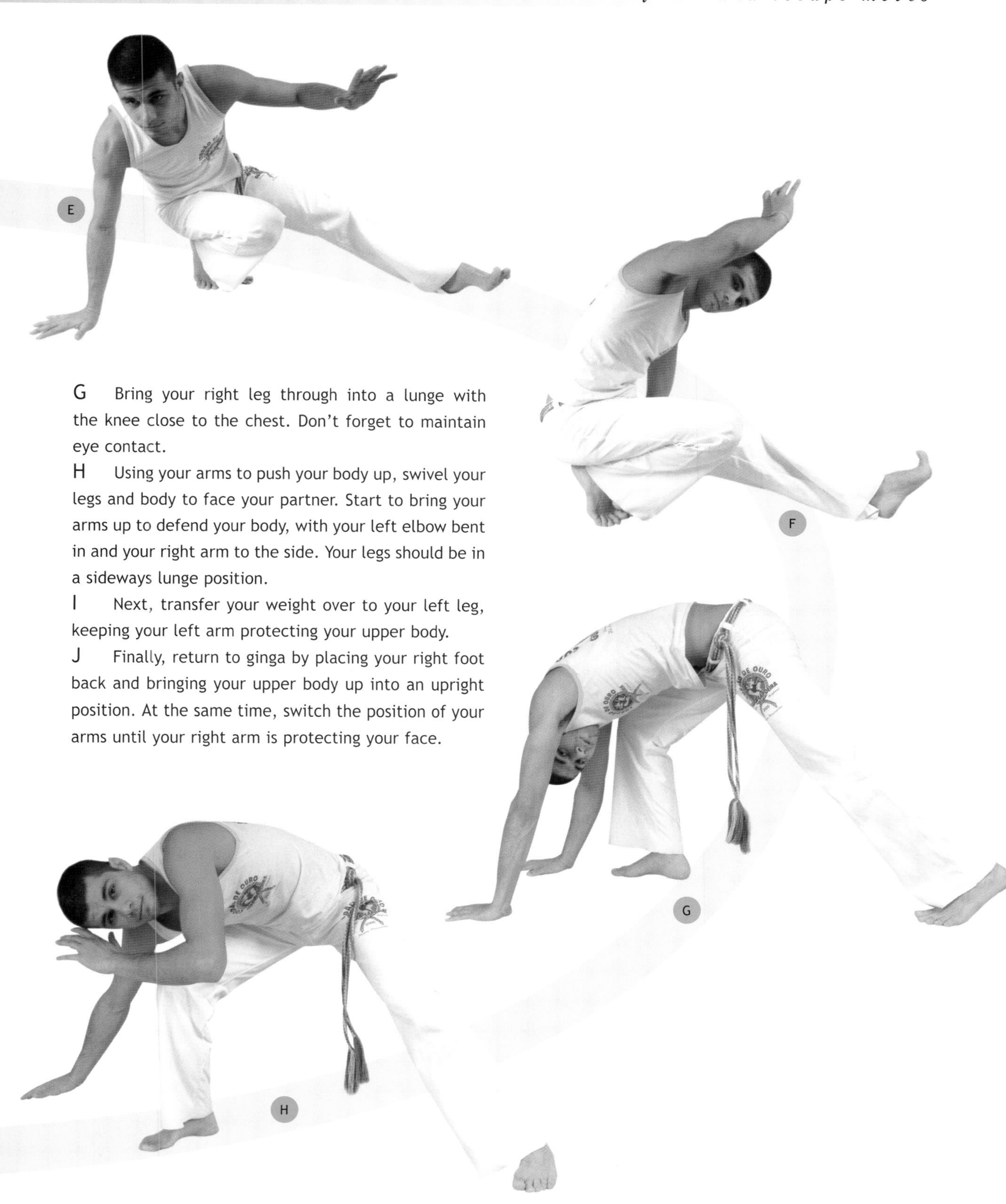

G Bring your right leg through into a lunge with the knee close to the chest. Don't forget to maintain eye contact.

H Using your arms to push your body up, swivel your legs and body to face your partner. Start to bring your arms up to defend your body, with your left elbow bent in and your right arm to the side. Your legs should be in a sideways lunge position.

I Next, transfer your weight over to your left leg, keeping your left arm protecting your upper body.

J Finally, return to ginga by placing your right foot back and bringing your upper body up into an upright position. At the same time, switch the position of your arms until your right arm is protecting your face.

Negativa recuada

The translation of the word 'recuada' means to go backwards. An important aspect of this defence move is that you are moving backwards in order to give yourself enough distance to counter-attack. You can use this position to gain momentum for another attack, making this negativa a very dynamic movement.

A Start from the ginga position, with your right foot forward and your left foot back. Your left arm should be up to protect your face with your right arm down to your right side.

B From the ginga position, start to lower yourself down to the floor by transferring the weight of your body onto your back foot. Keep your left arm protecting your face and maintain eye contact.

C Lower yourself fully to the ground and place your right hand on the floor for support. Your left heel should be off the floor, enabling you to sit on your back heel. Do not collapse into this position, but maintain a good balance. This will ensure that you are able to move easily if and when required.

D To return from the negativa position you can come back to ginga. You can reverse the movement by using your right hand to push yourself off the floor.

E Transferring your weight over the front leg, return to the full ginga position and continue play.

F Here is a front view of the negativa. Notice how the Capoeirista has not collapsed on to the back foot, but is supporting his balance and body weight through the back foot with a good, relaxed, supporting right hand.

C
D
F
E

Rolê

Rolê ('roll') is a movement that can be used to escape an attack and can also be used to move around the roda. Although it's direct translation means to roll, you are not actually rolling your body on the floor – you are using your arms and feet to move low to the ground in a continuous turning motion, stepping one leg over the other. You can link this move to other moves, making it a connecting transitional movement. It is similar to a negativa, but a negativa that allows you to move across the floor sideways, making this a very useful movement within the game.

A Start in a low position with your weight balanced on your back right heel. Your left leg should be relaxed to the front and your left arm placed on the floor supporting your balance. Your focus should be forward with your right arm folded across to protect the face.

B Pivot on your left leg and step over it with your right leg while you bring your right arm over your head and place it on the floor. Lift your right leg off the floor by bringing your heel in towards the back of your leg. Keep your focus towards your partner.

C Turn slightly further round to your left and place your right leg onto the floor, until you are in a lunge position with your left leg straight. Remember to keep your focus towards your partner.

D Transfer your weight on to the back foot from the lunge position and remove your left hand from the floor to fold in towards your chest. Your left leg stays out to the front with a relaxed knee.

E Shift your weight back to the start position by moving your arms – the left hand should be placed on the floor supporting the balance and the right arm folded in to protect your face.

Falling

The following movements will teach you how to fall correctly. It is important to practise these movements in order for you to begin to feel comfortable with falling on to your hands and feet. A Capoeirista should avoid any part of his body, other than the hands and feet, from touching the floor when he is falling. It is inevitable that while playing and training Capoeira you will fall. The importance of learning how to fall well is crucial in order to avoid injury, and it also enables the Capoeirista to continue his game smoothly. Due to the nature of the game we try to avoid staying on the floor after a fall, as a Capoeirista needs to be ready immediately to continue the game. There are no mats in Capoeira and you will often find yourself playing on hard surfaces, especially if, as an experienced Capoeirista, you are participating in a street roda. A fall can also often lead to another movement – if you recover quickly enough, you can manage to use the fall to spring into another move and the fall can pass unnoticed, bringing your game to another level. There is a famous phrase in the Capoeira world that is very relevant here: 'a good Capoeirista doesn't fall, but when he does he falls well'.

These falling techniques are used by everyone from beginners to the more advanced, but they require practise to enable you to support your body off the floor. To fall well can be considered as skilful as a successful attack within the Capoeira game, and a great fall can become a magical moment within the roda.

A

Queda de quatro

The queda de quatro (falling on all fours) teaches you how to fall on a strong base and it is a very safe way of falling. This is a movement that should never be taken for granted. Although you may appear vulnerable, you are actually in a very safe and strong position.

A From standing, go through to a squatting position.
B Fall backwards, throwing both arms back behind your body. Prepare your hands to land properly on the floor to avoid landing on your fingers.
C Land on both your hands at the same time and keep your elbows supple. Do not lock your arms as you land. Using your arms and your feet, keep your body off the floor, holding a forward focus throughout.

Queda de três

Queda de três (falling on to three supports) is mainly used when one leg has been swept away by your opponent, knocking you off balance. As you will have lost your base from the sweep, you need to use everything else you have available to land safely and efficiently.

A

A From the standing position, squat and throw yourself to the floor. Swing your right leg forward and both your arms back, preparing your hands for landing.
B Continue to throw your leg forward as you are falling.
C Land on your hands with your elbows soft and bring your right leg up to protect your body from attack. Your left knee will remain bent and your focus held forward. Keep your body off the floor and maintain your balance in this position to enable you to shift to another move at ease, without allowing your body to touch the floor. Remember to maintain eye contact with your partner.

B
C
D

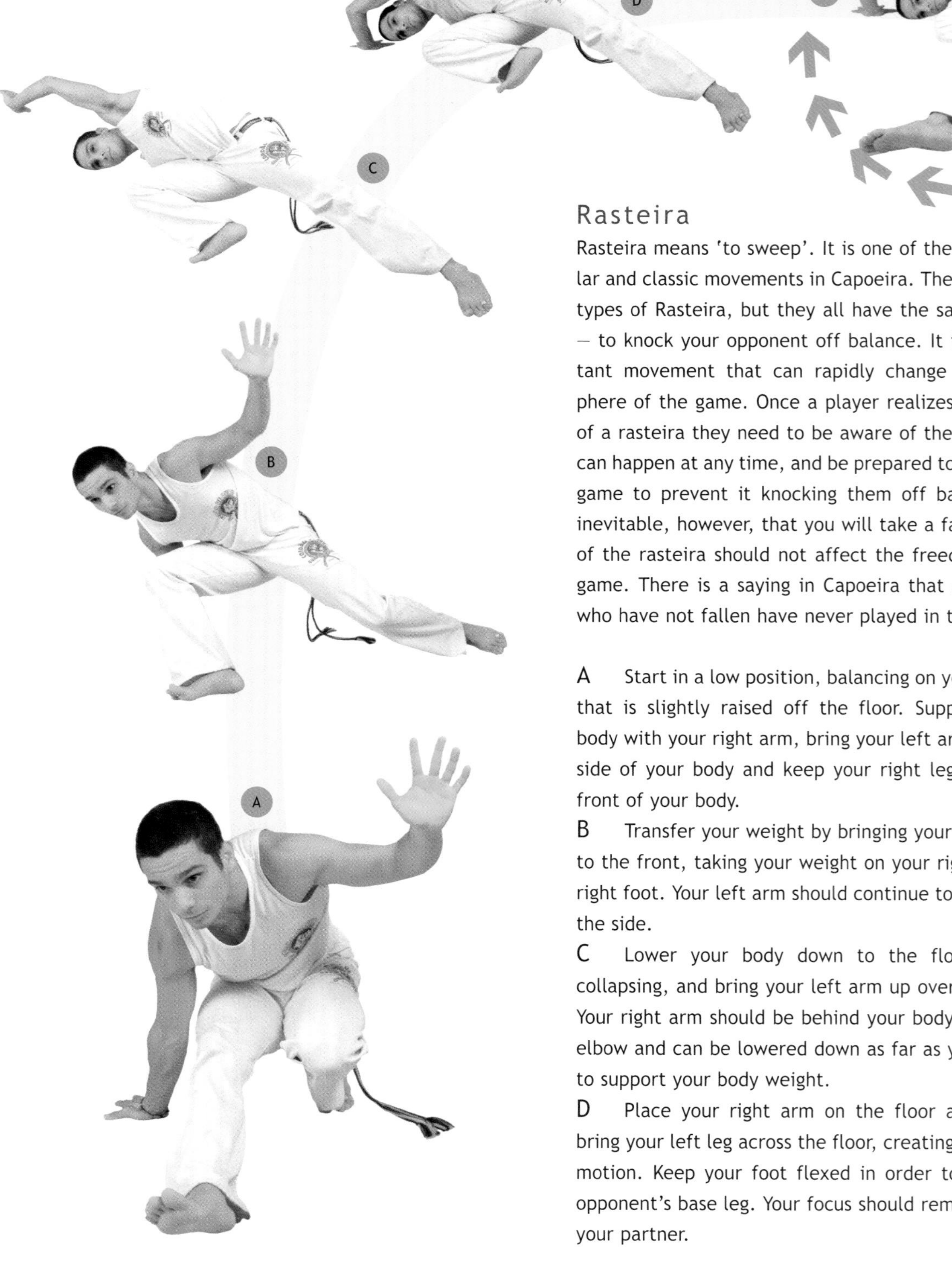

Rasteira

Rasteira means 'to sweep'. It is one of the most popular and classic movements in Capoeira. There are many types of Rasteira, but they all have the same purpose – to knock your opponent off balance. It is an important movement that can rapidly change the atmosphere of the game. Once a player realizes the danger of a rasteira they need to be aware of the fact that it can happen at any time, and be prepared to adapt their game to prevent it knocking them off balance. It is inevitable, however, that you will take a fall, and fear of the rasteira should not affect the freedom of your game. There is a saying in Capoeira that goes 'Those who have not fallen have never played in the roda'.

A Start in a low position, balancing on your left foot that is slightly raised off the floor. Supporting your body with your right arm, bring your left arm up to the side of your body and keep your right leg out to the front of your body.

B Transfer your weight by bringing your left leg out to the front, taking your weight on your right arm and right foot. Your left arm should continue to come up to the side.

C Lower your body down to the floor, without collapsing, and bring your left arm up over your head. Your right arm should be behind your body with a soft elbow and can be lowered down as far as you are able to support your body weight.

D Place your right arm on the floor and start to bring your left leg across the floor, creating a sweeping motion. Keep your foot flexed in order to hook your opponent's base leg. Your focus should remain towards your partner.

E Draw a complete half circle with the inside of your foot on the floor. Your foot should be flexed and your body off the floor the whole time. You are supporting yourself and controlling the movement with your arms, your right foot and the momentum of the rasteira.

F As your left leg completes the semi-circle, use your arms to push yourself up. Come up off the right leg until you are in a small lunge position with your hands on the floor in front of you. Look through your legs and arms at your partner.

G Swivel the position of your feet around to the front, back to a low position with your weight centred on your back left heel. Your right leg should be relaxed in front. Finally, release the right hand off the floor and fold it in to protect your face. You are now back to your starting position after completing the rasteira.

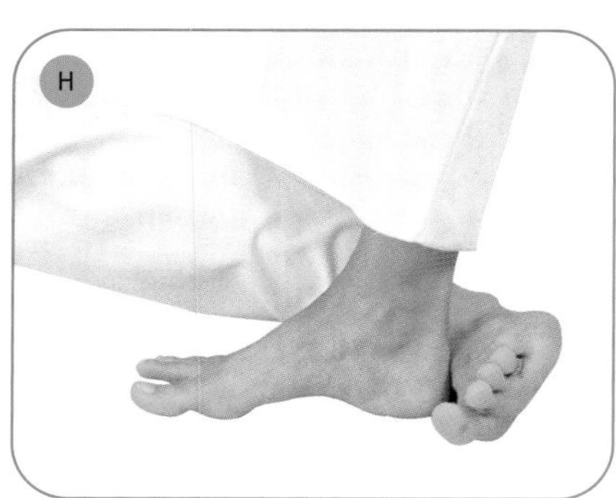

H This is a close-up of how the foot is used to hook the opponent's base leg with the rasteira. The flexed foot of the rasteira sweeps around to hook the foot of the base leg to sweep the opponent off balance.

I Rasteira in action: Capoeirista (i) has attacked her opponent with a kick. Capoeirista (ii) has seen the opportunity to use a rasteira with the intention of knocking Capoeirista (i) off her balance.

Tesoura

The tesoura ('scissors') is a traditional movement. When performed in a Regional game it can be quite an aggressive movement that can knock an opponent over by trapping both the legs, leaving no other option other than to fall safely. The following tesoura can typically be found in a game of Capoeira Angola where it can also be used as a trap, but allows the opponent more freedom of movement, adding fluidity and interaction to the game.

A Start in low position, balancing on your left foot that is slightly raised off the floor. Support your balance with the right arm on the floor, keep the right leg out to the front with a relaxed knee and fold your left arm in to protect your face.

B Bring your left arm up and over your body and place it on the floor above your head. At the same time pivot around to the right, using your right foot, and start to bring your left leg up and forward.

C Supporting your body weight with your arms, bring both knees in towards your chest, keeping a forward focus.

D Bring both your knees together into your chest until you reach a queda de rins position.

E Extend both your legs out to the floor. Using the support of your arms and feet, keep your hips slightly twisted to the right. Your left heel should be off the floor and your right foot beginning to plant itself fully on the floor.

F Push your body up with your arms and slide your feet along the floor, maintaining the direction of your hips and keeping your legs open. Look over your left shoulder to enable you to maintain eye contact in the tesoura position.

Golpes de Capoeira – Capoeira kicks

Golpes ('kicks') play a huge part in Capoeira. Your training for most of your attacks within the game will come in the form of a kick. There are many varieties of kick within Capoeira, with everything from frontal kicks, side kicks, diagonal kicks and spinning kicks, to over-head kicks and low-moving kicks. There is a kick for every direction, and they can come from many starting positions. Some of the kicks in Capoeira Regional were introduced by Mestre Bimba, inspired by other martial arts such as Savate. Many of the kicks, however, can only be found within the Capoeira game.

Kicks can also be incorporated into acrobatic moves. These may include kicking somebody from a bananeira (handstand), lowering the leg as the opponent approaches to attack with a cabeçada (head butt), or even a flying kick such as the parafuso (screw) which is a jumping combination of the armarda and martelo kicks.

There are kicks in Capoeira that are designed to attack your opponent from any angle. There are kicks to force your opponent backwards, sideways, in the air and to the floor. The delivery of kicks is very important, and the control of speed, height and distance will be gained through training regularly. A good Capoeirista can perform a kick without his opponent being able to anticipate where the kick is coming from; this type of deceit is common within the Capoeira game. It is important to take care that you have good control over your kicks when playing at this level, as many of these kicks can lead to serious injury. You need to be aware of where your leg is going and its intentions, so it is best to concentrate on and train in the more traditional ways of applying a kick before adding trickery. While training in these kicks, try to start off with a slow speed to achieve the correct technique – it is very important that you concentrate on the balance, control and base leg of the kick.

Bençâo

Bençâo ('to bless') is a frontal kick that is popular in both Capoeira Angola and Capoeira Regional. It can be used to push your opponent away from you and is usually aimed at the chest of your opponent.

A Start from the ginga position. Your left foot should be forward and your right foot back, with the right arm up protecting your face and your left arm down at your left side.

B Bring your right leg up from the back to the front by lifting your knee towards your chest. As you bring the knee up, switch over your arm position so that your left arm is in opposition to your knee, thus protecting your upper body. Keep your base leg knee bent to give yourself a good firm base with the supporting leg.

C Keeping your foot flexed, push your foot through the air until your kicking leg is fully extended. As you do this, tilt your pelvis forward and allow your upper body to counter-balance by tilting slightly backwards. Don't forget to maintain a forward focus throughout.

D The bençâo can be used to push your partner away from you in the roda. The Capoeirista in this example is placing her foot on her partner's chest.

E The Capoeirista shown here is receiving the bençâo and is escaping using the resistência (see pages 40–41).

F Here is the result of a strong, well-used bençâo. Notice how the pelvis is tilted forward and the supporting leg has a strong base.

Martelo

The martelo ('hammer') is a lateral kick that is quite similar to kicks used in other martial arts. It is a powerful kick that can be applied to the side of your opponent's upper body and head.

A Start from the ginga position. The left foot should be forward and the right foot back, with your right arm up protecting your face and the left arm by your left side.

B Swivel your left foot to the right, bringing your right knee up. Twist your pelvis around and switch the position of your arms with your left arm in opposition to the knee that is protecting the body.

C Extend your leg out with speed from the knee without allowing your knee to drop. Keep your left foot turned out and your supporting leg slightly bent for a strong base. Your upper body should tilt back slightly to counter-balance, but your shoulders should not fall back. Remember to maintain eye contact.

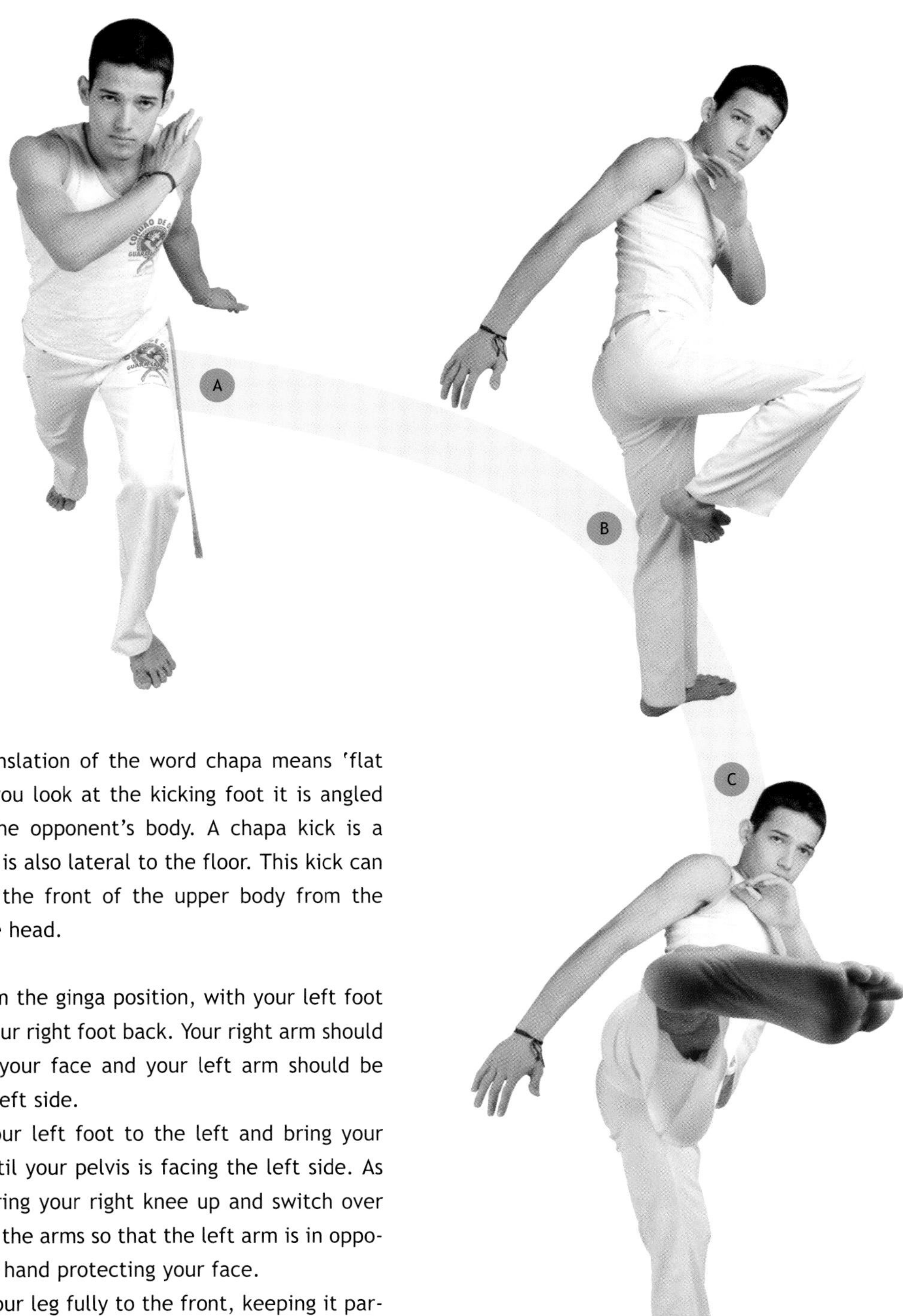

Chapa

The direct translation of the word chapa means 'flat surface' – if you look at the kicking foot it is angled flat towards the opponent's body. A chapa kick is a front kick that is also lateral to the floor. This kick can be applied to the front of the upper body from the stomach to the head.

A Start from the ginga position, with your left foot forward and your right foot back. Your right arm should be protecting your face and your left arm should be down by your left side.

B Swivel your left foot to the left and bring your body round until your pelvis is facing the left side. As you do this, bring your right knee up and switch over the position of the arms so that the left arm is in opposition with the hand protecting your face.

C Extend your leg fully to the front, keeping it parallel to the floor. Your body should be tilted back slightly to counter-balance the height of your kick, and your supporting left leg should remain turned out. The leg in the chapa does not unfold from the knee, but unlike the martelo the flexed foot pushes through the air.

Meia lua de frente

Meia lua de frente ('half moon to the front') is another classic kick of Capoeira, and earns its name by resembling the shape of a half moon. It is not only used to hit your opponent, but to also force them to go sideways and play lower to the floor. This kick adds fluidity to the game.

A Start from the ginga position with your right foot forward and your left foot back. Your left arm should be up protecting your face and your right arm down your right side.

B From the ginga position bring your left leg up and across the front of your body around hip height, with the foot flexed. While your leg comes up and across, the arms switch position with the right arm in opposition to the leg, protecting your body. The knee of your supporting leg remains soft for a strong base.

C Bring your kicking leg all the way across the front of your body to complete the shape of a half moon. Notice how the foot of the supporting leg is turned out – this should happen from the start of the kick.

D Once your half moon shape is complete, bring your kicking leg down from the end of the half moon shape to the right side of the body.

E To finish the kick and return to the ginga, start to fold your left leg back in from your knee.

F Start to place your left leg back into the ginga position by swivelling your body and supporting foot back to the front. Continue to fold your left leg down and back to the ginga position.

A Place your left foot, that has completed the meia lua de frente, back into the ginga position. You should now be ready to continue play.

D
E
F
G

Quexada

The quexada kick is a powerful and attractive move. It prepares you for other spinning kicks and, when practised continuously, can be used to improve the speed and control of your leg.

A Start from the ginga position. Your left foot should be forward and your right foot back with your right arm up protecting your face and your left arm down by your left side.

B Swivel your feet to the right and switch your arm position, with the left arm now protecting your face. Your legs should be in a wide squat position in preparation to kick.

C Shift your right leg forward to replace your left leg, which in turn lifts off the floor. Your arms should start to open out to switch position and your base foot should be turned out with a soft knee for a strong base.

D Fan your left leg up and out to the side, keeping the foot flexed and the body weight central so that you have a good balance. Your arms should now have switched and the right arm is folded in to protect the body.

E Open your leg fully to the side with your arms open ready to switch to the ginga position. Allow your left leg to fall straight from this position back to the ginga.

F This is a quexada in action. The Capoeirista that has just received the quexada is about to give her partner a rasteira. The firm base of the Capoeirista in the quexada will prevent him from falling.

Beija flor

The beija flor ('hummingbird') is a beautiful and impressive kick that can be executed with speed for an effective over head kick. The beija flor kick is more advanced and requires balance and control to use it efficiently in the roda. The kick is commonly used within Capoeira shows – the name is inspired by the shape of the movement as the leg can be compared with the beak of a hummingbird. Some groups may refer to this kick as aú batido, which means a cartwheel with the leg beating the air.

A BEIJA FLOR IN ACTION.

Spinning kicks

Spinning kicks can add speed and dynamics to your game and can be very exciting for the spectator. Spinning kicks vary in speed according to the rhythm of the game and a fast kick can also appear in a slow game.

Armada

This is a spinning kick unique to Capoeira. It develops a student's agility, balance and focus while they are turning at speed. It is a dynamic and visually impressive move.

A Start from the ginga position. Your right foot should be forward and your left foot back, with your left arm up protecting your face and your right arm down by your right side.

B Bring your left leg from the back of the ginga position to the side, keeping your arms in the same position and your body facing the front.

C Step onto your left leg and begin to turn yourself round towards the left shoulder. At this point your hips should be facing to the side. Your arms maintain the same position and your focus remains forward.

D Swivel yourself around towards your left shoulder. During the turn your right foot should be behind and your left foot in front. Your arms should have switched over, with your right arm protecting your face and your left arm to the side. Whip your head around to return focus to the front as quickly as possible.

E Bring the right leg forward and transfer the weight onto your right leg by lifting the left leg off the floor. Bring the focus forward as the upper body starts to face the front, with the left arm leading the way.

F Bring your left leg up from the floor with speed. Keep your base leg knee bent, as your left leg comes up. You are still in the middle of the continuous turn.

G Your left leg comes up from the right to the front of your body like an opening fan. Your base leg knee remains bent and your focus is forward.

H Your leg continues to carry to the side, with your base leg firmly planted on the floor. Your foot should be flexed.

I Your kicking leg comes from the side, straight down to the back to complete the kick by finishing in the ginga position.

D
E
F
G
H
I

Meia lua de compasso, or rabo de arraia

Meia lua de compasso ('half moon of the compass') is compared to a compass used in geometry because the base foot is planted on the floor and the other leg draws a circle in the air around you. In Capoeira Angola this kick is called the rabo de arraia ('tail of the stingray'). It is a low, grounded kick that can be quite dangerous when performed at speed. If you decide to do the meia lua de compasso with velocity be very careful as the speed of the heel coming around can seriously injure your opponent, especially if the opponent's reflexes are not fast enough to escape the oncoming kick. This kick should only be practised with speed when you are aware of your opponent's ability level and confident with your own control.

A Start from the ginga position. Your right foot should be forward and your left foot back with your left arm up protecting your face and your right arm down by your right side.

B Swivel your feet around to the left so that your hips are facing to the side. Your shoulders should face forward and your knees should be bent. Your focus should also remain forward.

C Place your hands on the floor so that your left arm is placed further back through your legs and your right arm is out to the front of your legs. Look through the small gap between your right arm and your right leg towards your partner – at this point the left leg should be straight. Keep your right leg bent in a kind of lunge position.

D Pivot around on your right leg and allow your hands to move around the floor to assist the pivot. Bring your left leg off the floor and begin to make a circle with the kick.

E Continue to pivot your base right leg and use the arms to bring yourself round with the head relaxed down. Keep the foot of the kicking leg flexed and your base leg knee bent. Don't forget to maintain eye contact with your opponent.

F Continue to move your leg around in a circle by pivoting your base right leg and using your arms on the floor. Notice how the eye contact has been maintained throughout.

G Bring yourself upright and lower your left leg to the back in the ginga position.

Meia lua de compasso with cocorinha

A   Capoeirista (i) applies the meia lua de compasso. Capoeirista (ii) uses the cocorinha to escape the oncoming kick.

Martelo de chão

Martelo de chão (a hammer kick on the floor) is a low kick that is not only used to kick, but also to force the opponent to escape, bringing colour and fluidity to the game. Due to the fact that Capoeira has lower, more grounded games, this kick is used when both of you are in a low game. It is a martelo kick that is adapted for the lower game.

A Start in a low position sitting over your left foot. The heel should be raised off the floor and you should be balanced on the ball of your foot. Keep your right leg out to the front with a soft knee. Place your right hand on the floor to support your balance and bring your left arm in to the air with the elbow bent. Keep your focus forwards.

B Lower yourself to the right by bending your right arm in so that the elbow comes in to the right side of your body. Bring your left arm further up above your head and start to move your body off your left heel.

C Lower your body fully to the right, tuck your elbow in above your hip and place your left arm on the floor in front of your head. Start to bring your back leg off the floor and don't forget to maintain eye contact in this position.

D As you bring your left leg up and over to the front, lower your head to the floor and keep the elbow well into the side of your body. Keep the left hand in a strong position on the floor to support yourself.

E Keep the same position and bring your left leg over, aiming towards the floor to the right.

F Allow your left leg to come down to the floor and bring yourself up by using your arms and legs. Keep the elbows supple and maintain eye contact throughout.

G Transfer your weight over to your left leg and straighten the right. Start to move your focus round to the right and bring your right arm off the floor to protect your face.

H Come up and swivel your legs and body to face the front in the ginga position with your arms and legs. Bring your right arm down to your side and your left arm up to protect your face.

I Martelo de chão ('martelo on the floor') in action.

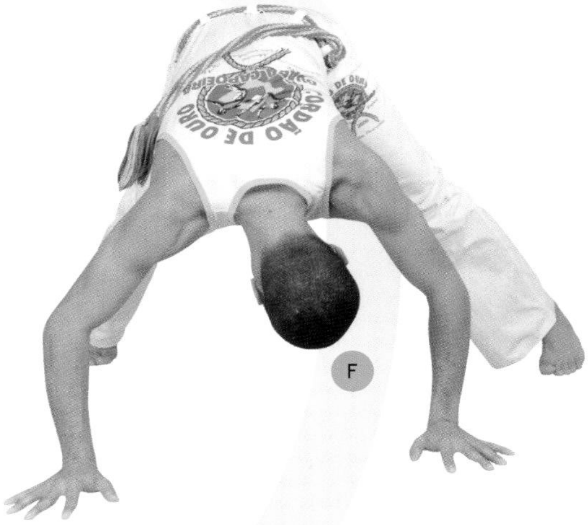

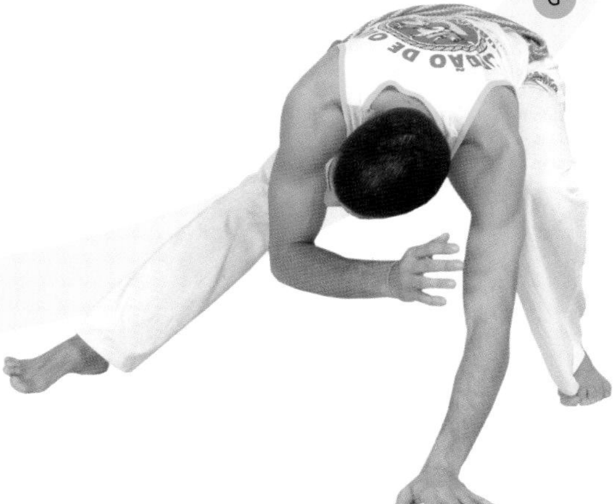

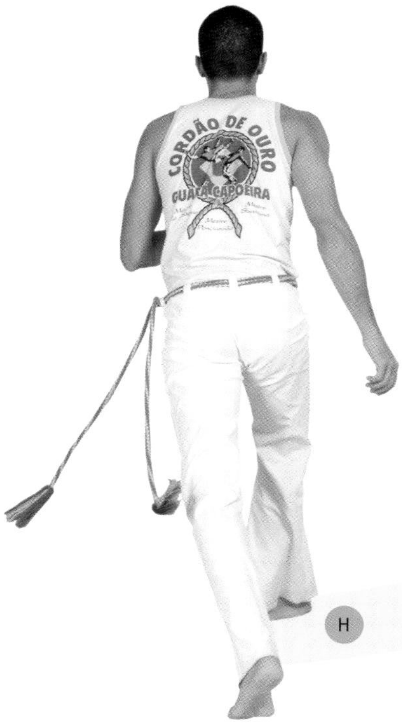

Training combinations

The following training combinations have been put together to enable you to incorporate some of the moves learnt in this chapter. By practising these sequences you will begin to gain an understanding of how to interact with your partner using attack and defence moves. These sequences are to be practised with two people and represent Capoeira in action.

Saida do berimbau

Saida do berimbau means 'leaving the berimbau'. At the start of a Capoeira game, both Capoeiristas crouch down in front of the berimbau. When they have been given permission to commence play they shake hands as a sign of respect and usually enter the roda performing the aú (cartwheel) movement.

A Crouch down in front of the berimbau and shake hands with your partner, making eye contact.

B Both Capoeiristas prepare to enter the roda with the aú movement, still maintaining eye contact.

C When performing the aú, both Capoeiristas need to be facing each other. Do not enter the roda with your back to your opponent.

D Both Capoeiristas descend from the aú movement into the ginga ready to commence the game. This is not a rule, but a suggestion.

Meia lua de frente with cocorinha

This basic combination will enable you to understand the use of cocorinha in escaping oncoming kicks. Training in the cocorinha with meia lua de frente will also start to prepare you for escaping spinning kicks, such as meia lua de compasso and armada.

A Starting from the ginga position, one of the Capoeiristas applies a meia lua de frente with the right leg.

B The meia lua de frente is completed while his opponent escapes it using a cocorinha.

C
D

Meia lua de frente with negativa recuada

As previously described, negativa recuada is an escape that enables you to move on the ground. This training exercise will teach you to escape by moving backwards while you are low to the ground.

A Both Capoeirista (i) and Capoeirista (ii) start mirroring each other from a ginga position.

B Both Capoeiristas ginga from left to right. During the ginga, Capoeirista (ii) begins to prepare himself to apply a meia lua de frente.

C Capoeirista (ii) applies a meia lua de frente. Capoeirista (i) goes down towards the floor with the left foot behind, bringing the left arm up to protect the face.

D Capoeirista (ii) completes the meia lua de frente. Capoeirista (i) escapes with a negativa recuarda.

Meia lua de compasso with cocorinha

In this combination you will gain an understanding of the power of meia lua de compasso. Make sure that you train for this exercise close together and that the kicking leg is not much higher than the head of the person that is defending. The person escaping with the cocorinha needs to come in close and under the kick, with their head just below the knee of the oncoming kick. The power of the kick is in the foot, so coming in closer will keep the defending Capoeirista in a safer place.

A Both Capoeiristas start by facing each other in a ginga position, with the left foot behind and the left arm folded across to protect the face.

B Both Capoeiristas step out to the side with the back leg.

C Capoeirista (ii) starts to apply the meia lua de compasso kick, turning anti-clockwise and maintaining eye contact. Capoeirista (i) goes into the cocorinha position, to escape the oncoming kick.

D–E Both Capoeiristas maintain their eye contact while Capoeirista (ii) completes the meia lua de compasso kick.

On completion of the meia lua de compasso kick, both Capoeiristas return to the ginga position.

Meia lua de compasso with rasteira

In this combination it is very important to ensure that your rasteira sweep moves in the same direction as the oncoming kick. A common mistake made by beginners is to move against the kick, thus leaving them vulnerable to attack.

A Capoeirista (ii) applies the meia lua de compasso. Capoeirista (i) escapes it and attacks Capoeirista (ii) by using the rasteira.

Meia lua de compasso training

This exercise should be practised in pairs starting at a moderate pace. It should be performed continuously and speeded up once you are comfortable with the move. It is common to feel dizzy while practising this move. If you experience dizziness, stop and rest before continuing with the exercise. It is important to warn your partner that you are about to stop as stopping abruptly can cause accidents. You should never underestimate the power of a meia lua de compasso – even when performed at a slow speed this kick can cause serious injuries. Timing and precision are vital in order to master this combination and to ensure your safety.

A The Capoeiristas start by facing each other in a ginga position, with the left foot behind and the left arm folded across to protect the face.

B Both Capoeiristas move into the preparation position for the meia lua de compasso, turning towards the back leg. Their hands are placed on the floor and eye contact is maintained.

C Capoeirista (ii) lifts his left leg off the floor and begins to execute the meia lua de compasso, turning anti-clockwise. Capoeirista (i) lifts his right leg off the floor, turning clockwise. Capoeirista (ii) is slightly further ahead in the movement than Capoeirista (i). As the leg of Capoeirista (ii) starts to pass over Capoeirista (i), Capoeirista (ii) follows with his meia lua de compasso.

Chapa with resistência

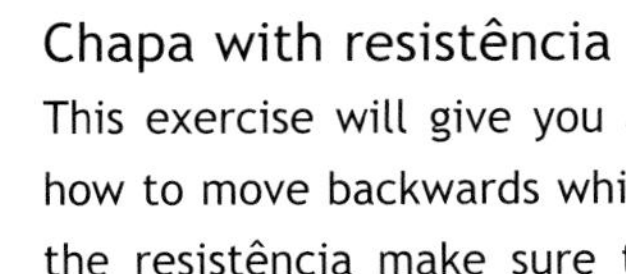

This exercise will give you a better understanding of how to move backwards while escaping. At the end of the resistência make sure that return to your game swiftly.

A Both Capoeiristas start by mirroring each other in the ginga position, Capoeirista (i) with the left leg back and Capoeirista (ii) with the right leg back.

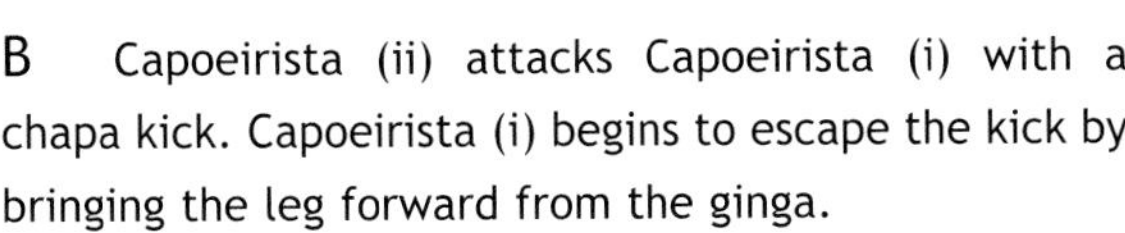

B Capoeirista (ii) attacks Capoeirista (i) with a chapa kick. Capoeirista (i) begins to escape the kick by bringing the leg forward from the ginga.

C Capoeirista (ii) fully extends the chapa kick towards her opponent's head. Capoeirsta (i) escapes the kick using the resistência. From this position Capoeirista (i) could quite easily go down to the floor and add a rasteira or simply connect a ground movement, such as a rolê, in order to continue the game.

Quexada training

This exercise should be practised in pairs starting at a moderate pace. It should be performed continuously and speeded up once you are comfortable with the move. This exercise is the best way to teach a Capoeirista to escape from fast spinning kicks, as your defence is not on the floor and you can counter-attack easily. It is also teaches you to move forward towards your opponent while he is kicking. Ensure that you always maintain eye contact and that your head is slightly backwards, which will make your esquiva more efficient.

A Both Capoeiristas start with their feet parallel with their left foot in front. They maintain eye contact even though they are facing different directions.

B Capoeirista (i) brings his right leg behind his left leg to prepare to apply the quexada. Capoeirista (ii) anticipates the kick by escaping with a small esquiva, transferring the weight over to his right leg.

C Capoeirista (i) applies the quexada kick with his left leg. Capoeirista (ii) escapes the kick with an esquiva to the right, leaning slightly backwards.

D Capoeirista (ii) starts his quexada kick by bringing his right leg forward towards the left leg. Capoeirista (i) begins to escape the kick, transferring the weight over to his left into a small esquiva.

E Capoeirista (ii) brings the leg higher into the quexada kick, maintaining eye contact. Capoeirista (i) lowers down into the esquiva. This low position also allows him to prepare to apply a quexada with his other leg. These quexadas can be practised continuously, and are a good way of building up velocity and improving your stamina.

Aú with cabeçada

This exercise should be practised in pairs, with each Capoeirista taking turns in each position. It is a great way to improve your ability to defend, as you are being attacked while you are upside down. You are not simply focusing on your balance, but also on your opponent who is moving in to headbutt you. Make sure that you keep close to your opponent and, once mastered, you will be able to add fluidity and interaction. Don't forget that when applied in a game, the cabeçada may be applied with some force, resulting in a fall. You must learn to recover from such a fall by using a queda de quatro or queda de três (pages 54–55).

A Start by facing your partner in a low, crouched down position.

B Capoeirista (ii) places his left hand on the floor and begins to transfer his weight over to the left side, bringing the right arm up.

C Capoeirista (ii) begins to move into the aú (cartwheel). Meanwhile, Capoeirista (i) places both hands on the floor and prepares himself to give a cabeçada (headbutt).

D Capoeirista (ii) performs the aú movement, keeping his focus forwards towards his partner. Capoeirista (i) moves in to give his partner a cabeçada in the stomach.

Bençāo, resistência with tesoura and aú

This is a more complex exercise involving the skills of both attack and defence. As you move into this combination, make sure you maintain eye contact. It is common for a beginner to focus on attack and defence, but to lose concentration and eye contact during the more fluid movements of the sequence, such as the tesoura and the aú. This is also a combination that starts high and finishes on the ground. Once complete don't forget to come up again into the ginga.

A Capoeirista (i) starts the benção kick by bringing his left leg up. Capoeirista (ii) begins to lean back in the resistência.

B Capoeirista (i) applies a full benção kick towards his opponent. Capoeirista (ii) goes back into a resistência to avoid the oncoming kick.

C Capoeirista (ii) lowers himself down to the floor to the queda de rins on his left elbow, with the right hand on the floor for support.

D Capoeirista (i) brings his left foot down from the benção. Capoeirista (ii) opens his legs into the tesoura position, looking back over his right shoulder towards his partner.

E Capoeirista (i) passes over the left leg of Capoeirista (ii), connecting into the aú movement. Capoeirista (ii) begins to raise his body off the floor from the tesoura.

F Capoeirista (i) executes the aú movement over the left leg of Capoeirista (ii). Both Capoeiristas have maintained eye contact throughout, and complete their movements by returning to the ginga position. Note that by the end of this sequence they have changed sides.

Martelo with rasteira em pé

This exercise trains you for the rasteira from a standing position. The rasteira em pé ('sweep from standing') simply means that the rasteira does not go all the way to the floor. This move should be practised in the same direction as the oncoming kick. Both Capoeiristas should take turns to practise both of the movements on each side.

A Both Capoeiristas start in the ginga position. Capoeirista (i) has his left leg back and Capoeirista (ii) is mirroring his partner with his right leg back.

B Capoeirista (ii) brings his back leg from the ginga position and begins to apply the martelo kick with his right leg. Capoeirista (i) brings his back leg from the ginga position and begins to apply a rasteira to the base leg of Capoeirista (ii).

C Capoeirista (ii) completes the martelo kick while Capoeirista (i) knocks the base leg of Capoeirista (ii) with the rasteira, with the intention of taking him off balance.

Both Capoeiristas return to the ginga position. From here the Capoeiristas ginga to change legs and repeat the exercise with the other leg.

Final notes on training combinations

As mentioned in the previous pages, maintaining eye contact is an important part of your training. I normally tell my students that if you are not focusing on each other and interacting, there is no point in practising combinations. Before beginning the sequences, ensure that both you and your partner are ready by doing some of the exercises shown in the warm-up section (pages 26–33). This can be followed by a five minute ginga. Once you have learned the combinations you should start to train in a more playful way by mixing, creating and improvising. These combinations provide a bridge from exercises to the actual game. Use the steps that come naturally to you and do not simply use the moves as though they are dance steps. You are not engaging in a solo performance – the most important part of the game is the interaction.

Strength, balance and flexibility

The training exercises in this book will improve your strength, balance and flexibility. In the art of Capoeira these three components put together will increase your range of movement and allow you to move more freely within your game, while also improving your stamina. Stamina is an important asset within the roda, enabling you to play to the best of your ability for longer periods. Flexibility, meanwhile, will improve the efficiency of attacks, escapes and the execution of advanced moves. Balance will add control and beauty to the execution of your moves and minimize the possibility of falling. Strength will decrease the possibility of injury and is the basis of flexibility, precision and balance. A well-rounded Capoeirista will strive to attain a good level of balance, strength and flexibility and will not neglect any of these three aspects of training.

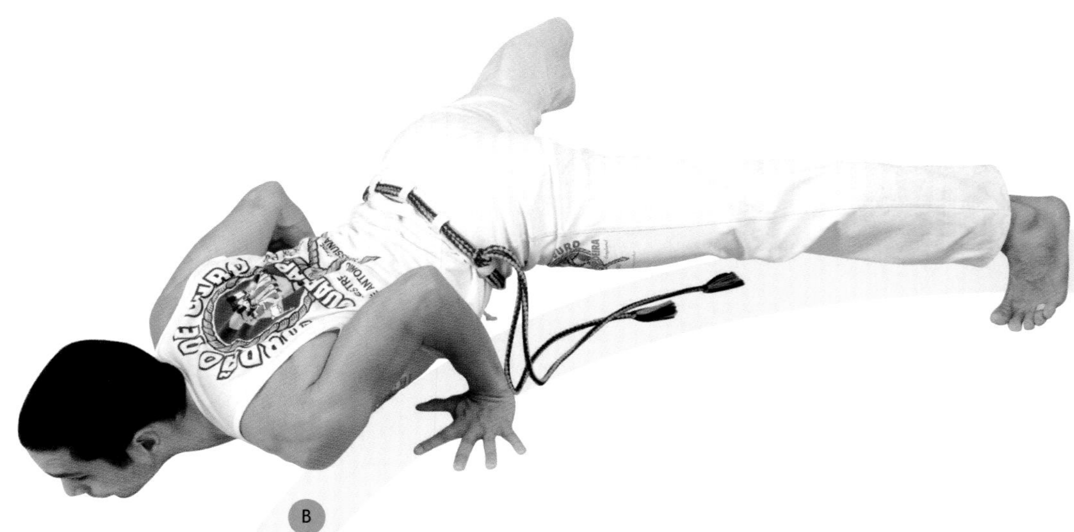

Excercises to strengthen the upper body

Mergulho

You will find mergulho ('to dive') used in most Capoeira classes. It may seem impossible at first, but with time you will see an improvement in your upper body strength and flexibility.

A Start on all fours with your legs open wide and your knees straight.

B Lower yourself down to the floor, keeping your elbows in and your upper body slightly off the ground. Do not rest your body on the floor.

C Straighten your elbows and push your upper back up.

D Lower your upper body back down to the floor and then push yourself back up with your arms.

Return to the starting position, stretching out your lower back. Repeat this movement several times.

Exercise for queda de rins

Many movements within Capoeira involve leaning and balancing with your elbow in the side of your body. This can feel uncomfortable at first, but once you gain sufficient upper body strength to support yourself with the elbow in the correct position, you will find it more beneficial to assist you in perfecting the moves. Queda de rins ('fall onto the kidneys') is demanding, but with dedication and daily practise you will soon feel the benefits. It will help to increase your movement facility and bring an increased fluidity to your game.

A Start with your legs apart and your hands on the floor in front of your body, keeping your back straight.
B Move your weight over to your arms as you start to bend in the right knee.
C As you continue to bend your right knee in, keep the leg straight. Lower your upper body weight to the floor by bending your elbows, bringing your right elbow into your right side just above your right hip. As you lower yourself down turn your head to the left. Do not allow any part of your body to touch the floor. Hold this position for a couple of seconds.
D Return to the starting position by using your arms to push your body away from the floor and straighten your right knee. Once returned to the starting position, repeat the exercise on the other side.

Ponte training

Ponte ('bridge') is a basic movement that can be performed on its own. Practising ponte will improve a whole range of movements and helps to add fluidity to your game. There are many moves within Capoeira that will benefit from training in the ponte.

A Lie flat on the floor with your knees bent and your feet shoulder width apart. Place your hands up above your head with your palms flat on the floor and your fingers pointing towards your shoulders.

B Push your hands into the floor and raise your pelvis to the ceiling. Start to bring your head and body off the floor.

C Achieve the full ponte by using your arms to push your pelvis up as far as you can, allow your head to relax back and your legs to straighten. Don't forget to keep the knees soft.

Backbend training

This movement must be practised with two people and will help you to gain confidence in moving while you are upside down. It will also improve your judgment as to when your hands should reach the floor in backwards movements and will increase your control, balance and flexibility.

A Capoeirista (i) secures his partner by the wrists with a wide stance and relaxed knees. Capoeirista (ii) stands straight, lifting her arms above her head.

B Capoeirista (i) brings his upper body forward, keeping his knees bent and securing his partner firmly by her wrists. Capoeirista (ii) allows her partner to lift her body back as he bends forward. At this point her feet are coming off the floor.

C Capoeirista (i) keeps hold of the wrists and, bending the knees, brings the upper body down to the floor and places his partner's hands on the floor.

D Capoeirista (ii) allows Capoeirista (i) to place her hands on the floor and start to lift her left leg up.

E Capoeirista (i) straightens his legs and allows his partner to complete her movement. Capoeirista (ii) now has her focus forward and is allowing her left leg to go towards the floor, with her lower back still resting on her partner for support. Capoeirista (i), although supporting his partner less, must be aware of his partner's balance before letting go. Capoeirista (ii) allows her left foot to find the floor, and brings the rest of her body over. At this point her fellow Capoeirista has let go, but is still close by.

F Capoeirista (ii) brings both her feet to the floor, bringing her legs over and finishing with the feet parallel.

G Both Capoeiristas finish by rolling through the spine to a standing position.

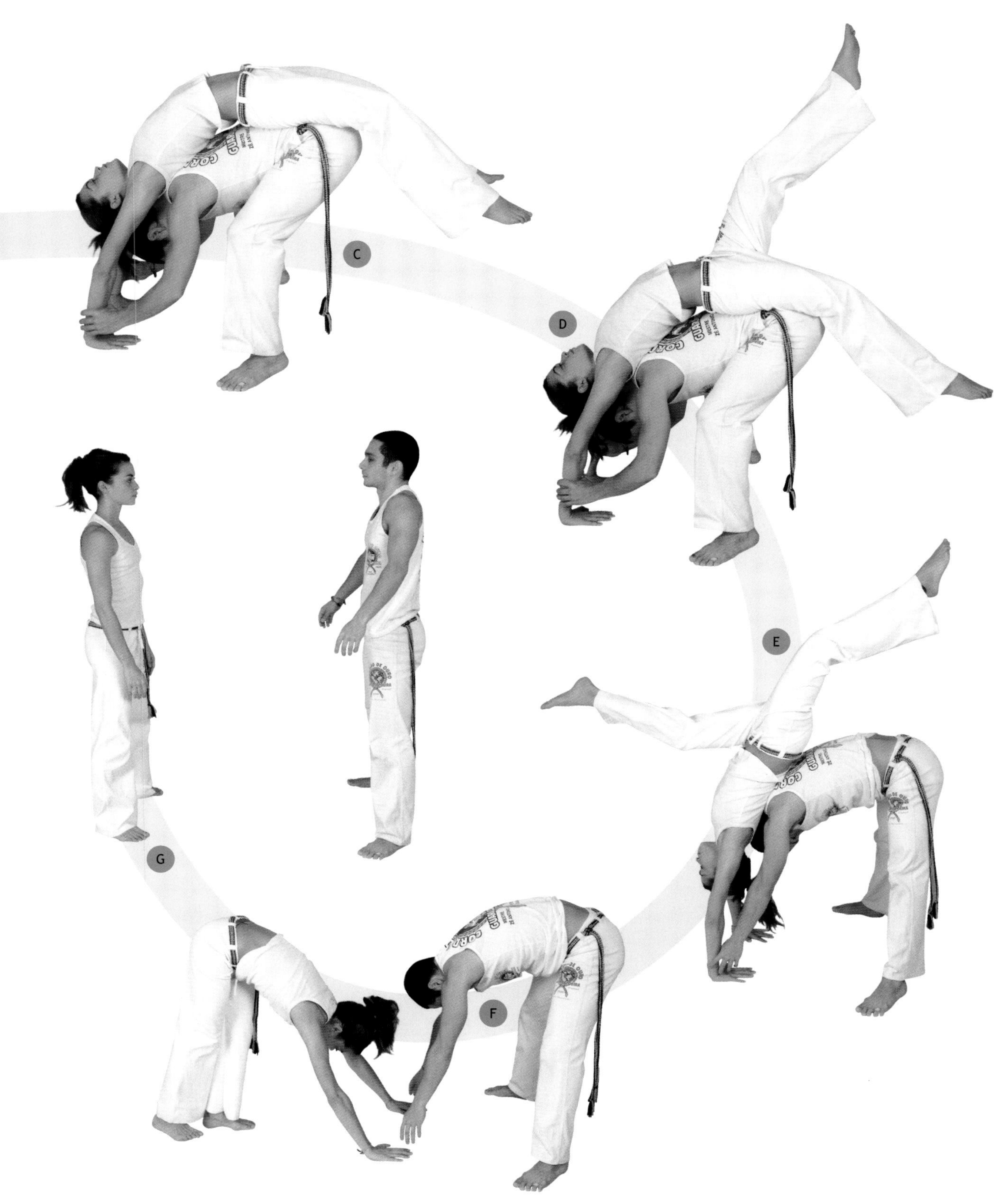
C
D
E
F
G

Practising the bananeira

There are many forms of the bananeira (handstand). Once you have mastered the simple bananeira you can be creative and play around with your balance. Capoeiristas who are comfortable with their balance can perform the bananeira with one hand. This in turn can evolve, with the Capoeirista jumping and turning on one hand. This turn is referred to as pião de mão ('turn on one hand'). It is also quite common for Capoeiristas to walk around the roda on their hands. There are also bananeiras that involve leaning the body over in different directions, such as performing a back bend in the bananeira. These are impressive balances and a great demonstration of strength and flexibility.

Always keep the focus forward, as more often than not there will be a cabeçada (headbutt) coming your way to test your balance. Cabeçada is the chosen mode of attack when performing a bananeira as it is bad etiquette to kick your opponent's arms, body or head while they are balancing in this move.

For a simple bananeira you can start by practising with a partner holding your legs for support and balance, or against a wall. Once you start to practise the bananeira alone, take care that there is nobody behind you and that you have plenty of space.

Bananeira training exercise

A Capoeirista (ii) starts in a standing position holding his partner by the right ankle. Capoeirista (i) keeps both hands on the floor, looking towards his partner with the right leg lifted off the floor.

B Capoeirista (ii) comes in towards his partner and secures his partner's ankle with both hands.

C Capoeirista (i) lifts his left leg off the floor while his partner is securing his right leg, taking the weight into both hands on the floor.

D Capoeirista (i) brings his left leg towards the ceiling, while keeping his focus towards his partner.

E Capoeirista (i) straightens his left leg towards the ceiling and concentrates on his balance in this position, while his partner keeps him on balance by securing his right leg. When the balance is found his partner can remove his grip to test the balance, but be ready to catch his partner if he starts to fall. To release, Capoeirista (i) returns his left leg to the floor.

F An important factor of the bananeira is to focus forward towards your partner. Many people start to practise it looking at the floor, but it is vital that you start to train for the bananeira with your head relaxed and the top of your head pointing towards the floor. This way you will still be able to see what is happening within the game.

More creative examples of the bananeira

It is likely that you will see many different varieties of bananeiras being performed by the more advanced students within the roda. Here are a few examples of bananeiras taking different forms within the balance.

A This bananeira involves excellent balance and shoulder strength.

B The lower part of the body has been lowered down from the lower back and the left leg kept bent in while the right leg is stretched out towards the floor.

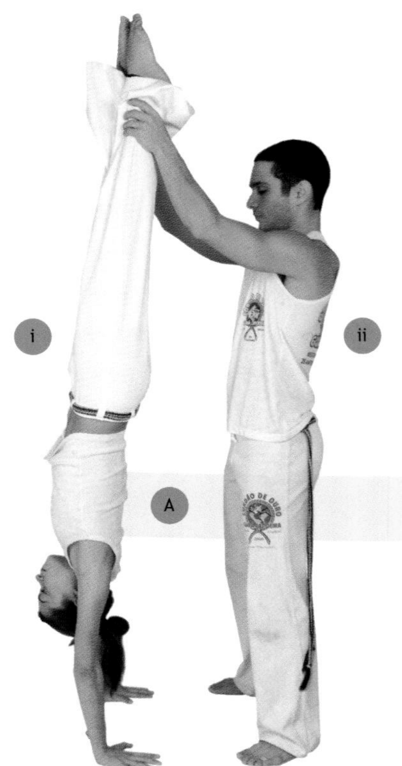

Ponte de bananeira (a bridge from a handstand)

A   Capoeirista (i) goes up into a handstand, keeping her focus forwards. Capoeirista (ii) secures his partner by holding both ankles.

B   Capoeirista (ii) then turns around until he is back to back with his partner, continuing to secure his partner's ankles firmly.

C   Capoeirista (ii) begins to squat in a wide stance. As he is squatting he takes the weight of his partner's body over his back with a firm grip, being sure to keep his partner on balance. It is very important that he keeps a straight back as he goes down and is in a deep squat to avoid back injury. You should never arch your lower back in this position.

D   As Capoeirista (ii) bends forward, he brings his partner over his back. The hands of Capoeirista (i) leave the floor and she allows her partner to place her feet on the floor.

E   Capoeirista (i) gains her balance with the help of her partner and then brings her upper body up to a standing position to complete the movement.

E

Aú de cabeça

Aú de cabeça ('cartwheel on the head') is a type of cartwheel, but because you have your head on the floor, it is classed as a ground movement rather than an acrobatic movement. Aú de cabeça is a common movement within a game of Capoeira Angola and the Muidinho game of Cordão de Ouro. It is a beautiful movement that an advanced student can perform by removing their hands from the floor and balancing on the top of their head. It is also a stylish movement, which, when added to your game, will allow you to move around the roda.

A Start in a low position with your weight resting on your back left foot and your right leg out to the front. Supporting your balance with your right hand on the floor, bring up your left arm to the side, keeping your focus forward.

B On your right foot, pivot around to the right, bringing your back foot off the floor and allowing the left arm to come over and join your right hand on the floor. Don't forget to keep your focus towards your partner.

C Place the top of your head on the floor and bend your elbows so that your arms are in a good position to support your body. Continue to lift your left leg off the floor.

D Balancing on your head, bring your left leg up and at the same time start to bring your right leg off the floor.

(Continued)

E
F

(Continued)

E Bring your right foot off the floor, using your arms and your head to maintain a steady balance.

F—G Bring your left foot down to the floor first and then allow the right foot to follow to finish the movement.

H As your right foot comes down to the floor, swivel your feet and body to face the front by bringing your right foot to the back. Pivot on your back foot to return to the starting position, with your right foot behind you and your left foot in front. It is important that you maintain eye contact with your partner throughout.

G

THE MUSIC

Music is a central and essential part of Capoeira, setting it apart from other martial arts. It is a traditional part of Capoeira that most groups strive to uphold. It is perhaps the use of music within Capoeira that leads to the common confusion as to whether or not it is a fight or a dance. The music sets the tempo and style of the roda, be it an Angola game or a fast and dynamic Regional-style fight. Music within Capoeira encourages the fluid movements of the Capoeirista and enables them to keep time. The use of music also encourages a sense of belonging, where students sing together as they watch others play. Within the roda, work and commitments can be left outside – the powerful music of Capoeira helps students to do this. Without the music of the bateria (orchestra) one cannot experience true Capoeira.

The bateria is at the heart of every roda. It is usually made up of three main instruments: the berimbau (a monochordal musical bow), the pandeiro (tambourine) and the atabaque (drum).

The berimbau

The berimbau is sometimes referred to as the soul of Capoeira, and is often used as the symbol of the art. Mestres have been known to say that the berimbau is the real mestre of the roda, and its importance cannot be underestimated within Capoeira. Learning to play the berimbau is an important part of a Capoeirista's training, especially for those aiming to progress in the art.

The emergence of the berimbau within Capoeira is in dispute, but what is certain is that it originated from Africa. This musical bow was originally used to accompany storytelling, poetry and chants. The berimbau is one of the oldest known instruments. Modern versions are made up of a single string from the wire of a used car tyre, which is attached to a wooden bow. The bow is made from biriba, a strong yet flexible wood that provides a good shape and powerful sound. A cabaça (a hollowed gourd) is attached to the bottom of the bow and serves to amplify the sound.

THE THREE BERIMBAUS: VIOLA (TOP), MEDIO (MIDDLE) AND GUNGA OR BERRA BOI (BOTTOM), WITH CABAÇAS THAT INCREASE IN SIZE.

opposite MESTRE PONCIANINHO PLAYS THE ATABAQUE, A TALL DRUM MADE FROM COW SKIN.

BARIS YAZAR PERFORMS A 'PARAFUSO' FLYING KICK. PARAFUSO MEANS 'TWIST', OR 'SCREW'.